W9-DAJ-583

Praise for...

Fashioned for Intimacy

—⟨⟨⟨—

Our culture of growing gender confusion is not only desperate to
know that there is, indeed, a Creator, but that He has a wise and
original design and purpose for men and women.
Fashioned for Intimacy explains God's beautiful blueprint.
It is a lamp of truth in a dark forest of wrong ideas.

Vonette Z. Bright
COFOUNDER, CAMPUS CRUSADE FOR CHRIST INTERNATIONAL
FOUNDER AND DIRECTOR, WOMEN TODAY INTERNATIONAL
ORLANDO, FLORIDA

Tender, inspiring and clear. From the opening pages, I knew
I was reading a classic I would read to my children.

John Dawson
FOUNDER, INTERNATIONAL RECONCILIATION COALITION
SUNLAND, CALIFORNIA

Fashioned for Intimacy is clearly at the heart of what God is
saying and doing in the Church today to restore the most
foundational of relationships—that between men and women
in the sanctity of marriage. This is a book every husband
ought to read *with* his wife.

Dick Eastman
INTERNATIONAL PRESIDENT, EVERY HOME FOR CHRIST
COLORADO SPRINGS, COLORADO

A sacred torch is being carried by God's angels—in the heat of its fire, spiritual purity and healing are emerging between pastors, denominations and cultures. With *Fashioned for Intimacy*, Jane Hansen and Marie Powers bring this holy flame to the fallen relationship between men and women.

Francis Frangipane
SENIOR PASTOR, RIVER OF LIFE MINISTRIES
CEDAR RAPIDS, IOWA

Cutting edge in its impact and full of revelation, *Fashioned for Intimacy* will bring healing to marriages and relationships in the Church. I highly recommend it to the whole Body of Christ.

Cindy Jacobs
COFOUNDER, GENERALS OF INTERCESSION
COLORADO SPRINGS, COLORADO

How do twenty-first century leaders avoid the rocky slopes of sex dominance and the wailing valleys of women indentured forever into unilateral submission? Jane Hansen and Marie Powers do it with uncommon grace. It is clear that the authors pay no dues to political correctness as defined by either the political left or right. *Fashioned for Intimacy* is literally "aglow" with gentle encouragement to women and men alike. Created together, men and women need each other in restored respect, mutual submission and celebrative dialogue. Jesus is coming soon, and the sounds you hear are wedding music!

Donald M. Joy, Ph.D.
PROFESSOR OF HUMAN DEVELOPMENT AND FAMILY STUDIES
ASBURY THEOLOGICAL SEMINARY
WILMORE, KENTUCKY

In a time when a massive assault is coming against the family, books like this one will help to turn the tide of battle. *Fashioned for Intimacy* is must reading for men and women alike.

Rick Joyner
MORNINGSTAR PUBLICATIONS AND MINISTRIES
CHARLOTTE, NORTH CAROLINA

In *Fashioned for Intimacy*, Jane Hansen and Marie Powers inspire fresh insight and a renewed vision of biblical intimacy between men and women. The authors display masterful storytelling skill and share a deep understanding of the Father's desire to lead the male/female relationship from isolation to reconciliation, from reconciliation to restoration and from restoration to oneness.

Steve L. Shanklin
NATIONAL NETWORK PRAYER MANAGER, PROMISE KEEPERS
DENVER, COLORADO

Jane Hansen and Marie Powers have done the Body of Christ an immeasurable service with this balanced, well-written book. They have taken what is often a highly volatile and divisive subject and, with incredible insight and accurate scholarship, cut through the religious fog and human traditions. *Fashioned for Intimacy* will radically impact the Body of Christ! I highly recommend it to both men and women.

Dutch Sheets
PASTOR, SPRINGS HARVEST FELLOWSHIP
COLORADO SPRINGS, COLORADO

Unless relationships between men and women are restored to God's original design, there is little hope we will live to see the outpouring of God's Spirit for which we have been fervently praying. In this remarkable book, Jane Hansen and Marie Powers lay an awesome foundation, pointing us and moving us in that direction. *Fashioned for Intimacy* should be required bedtime reading for every Christian couple.

C. Peter Wagner

FULLER THEOLOGICAL SEMINARY
COLORADO SPRINGS, COLORADO

Fashioned for Intimacy

—⁓—

Reconciling Men and Women to God's Original Design

Jane Hansen
with Marie Powers

Regal

A Division of Gospel Light
Ventura, California, U.S.A.

Published by Regal Books
A Division of Gospel Light
Ventura, California, U.S.A.
Printed in U.S.A.

Regal Books is a ministry of Gospel Light, an evangelical Christian publisher dedicated to serving the local church. We believe God's vision for Gospel Light is to provide church leaders with biblical, user-friendly materials that will help them evangelize, disciple and minister to children, youth and families.

It is our prayer that this Regal book will help you discover biblical truth for your own life and help you meet the needs of others. May God richly bless you.

For a free catalog of resources from Regal Books/Gospel Light please contact your Christian supplier or call 1-800-4-GOSPEL.

All Scripture quotations, unless otherwise indicated, are taken from the *New King James Version.* Copyright © 1979, 1980, 1982 by Thomas Nelson, Inc. Publishers. Used by permission. All rights reserved.

Other versions used are:
AMP. N.T.—Scripture quotations are taken from the *Amplified New Testament,* copyright © 1954, 1958, 1987 by The Lockman Foundation. Used by permission.
AMP. O.T.—From *The Amplified Bible, Old Testament.* Copyright © 1965, 1987 by The Zondervan Corporation. Used by permission.
KJV—*King James Version.* Authorized King James Version.
The Message—*The New Testament in Contemporary English* by Eugene H. Peterson, © 1994. NavPress, Colorado Springs, Colorado.
The Bible: James Moffatt Translation by James A. R. Moffatt. Copyright © 1922, 1924, 1925, 1926, 1935 by Harper Collins San Francisco. Copyright 1950, 1952, 1953, 1954 by James A. R. Moffatt. Printed in the United States of America.
NASB—Scripture taken from the *New American Standard Bible,* © 1960, 1962, 1963, 1968, 1971, 1972, 1973, 1975, 1977 by The Lockman Foundation. Used by permission.
NIV—Scripture quotations are taken from the *Holy Bible, New International Version®. NIV®.* Copyright © 1973, 1978, 1984 by International Bible Society. Used by permission of Zondervan Publishing House. All rights reserved.
PHILLIPS—*The New Testament in Modern English,* Revised Edition, J. B. Phillips, Translator. © J. B. Phillips 1958, 1960, 1972. Used by permission of Macmillan Publishing Co., Inc., 866 Third Avenue, New York, NY 10022.
TLB—Verses marked (*TLB*) are taken from *The Living Bible* © 1971. Used by permission of Tyndale House Publishers, Inc., Wheaton, IL 60189. All rights reserved.

© Copyright 1997 by Jane Hansen. All rights reserved.

Cover Design by Barbara LeVan Fisher • Interior Design by Britt Rocchio • Edited by Kathi Mills and Virginia Woodard

Library of Congress Cataloging-in-Publication Data
Hansen, Jane.
    Fashioned for intimacy / Jane Hansen.
        p. cm.
    Includes bibliographical references.
    ISBN 0-8307-2064-2 (trade paper)
    1. Intimacy (Psychology—Reiligious aspects—Christianity. 2. Man-woman relationships—Religious aspects—Christianity. 3. Marriage-Religious aspects—Christianity. I. Title.
BV4597.53.I55H37 1997   97-29869
248.8'44—dc21   CIP

1 2 3 4 5 6 7 8 9 10 11 12 13 14 15 16 17 18 19 20 / 04 03 02 01 00 99 98 97

Rights for publishing this book in other languages are contracted by Gospel Literature International (GLINT). GLINT also provides technical help for the adaptation, translation and publishing of Bible study resources and books in scores of languages worldwide. For further information, contact GLINT, P.O. Box 4060, Ontario, CA 91761-1003, U.S.A., or the publisher.

Contents

—⟋⟋⟋—

"He is restoring the house, the dwelling place of the Lord, that He might come to that house and fill it with His glory."

"Because God is a Father, has the nature of a Father and is alone the source of all goodness, He wanted to reproduce Himself and fill the earth with His own image—all that He is."

"From the moment God conceived in His mind to create a family for Himself—before the first stars of humanity's earthly home were hung in the sky, knowing all it would cost Him—His plan was finished."

"When God placed Adam in the garden, telling him to guard and protect it, God did not intend that Adam should do so in his own strength."

Acknowledgments

—◊—

I want to acknowledge those who have walked alongside me through the process of writing this book to encourage, to help, to pray; those who have "heard the sound."

Thanks to Jennie Newbrough who began telling me five years ago, "You need to write this word!" She has travailed in prayer to bring this project to birth. Thanks to Diane Moder, whom God has also used to help hold up my arms. Karen Anderson, editor at Aglow, has been a wonderful help to me. Laurie Lischke, Lorene Carlson, Kay Rogers, Diane Fink and Pat Gaines are others who have been there for me, lending their support, love and prayers in so many ways. Thanks to Carol Greenwood, friend and skilled author, for her special touch on the falcon story.

A word of appreciation to Kathi Mills, my Regal editor; Kyle Duncan, Bill Greig III and their staff at Regal Books with whom it has been so great to work.

Then, to my faithful, understanding, caring husband and family, who so generously allowed me the time needed to write, my deep and heartfelt gratitude and love.

Finally, to my dear friend Marie Powers who has coauthored this work. I want to say thank you for your diligence, care and faithfulness in helping to give expression to what we both see as the heart of God for His Church. May God use this word to bring much-needed healing and restoration to the Body of Christ as He continues to prepare us for His return.

With all my heart, I give thanks to each one of you, and to the Lord for His incredible love, boundless mercy and manifold wisdom.

Jane Hansen
Edmonds, Washington, June 1997

Introduction

—∞—

Heaven must receive [and retain] [Him] until

the time for the complete restoration

of all that God spoke.

ACTS 3:21 *(AMP.)*

Many things are being restored in our day. Some refer to what is happening as the reconciliation movement, "a movement that is confronting important strongholds such as racism, and other roots of division."[1]

The Holy Spirit is restoring our vision, opening our eyes to see as never before: areas of prejudice, places we have hurt and wounded one another and mind-sets that have caused our hearts to be closed to one another. What a tremendous outpouring of grace we are experiencing as the Holy Spirit prepares the family of God for the return of Christ!

Our introductory Scripture verse indicates that all things will be restored prior to Jesus' release from heaven to return to earth. We understand this does not mean that the earth and all the ills of the world will be restored and somehow miraculously made right. Isaiah 60:2 states that "darkness shall cover the earth, and deep darkness the people." In this same passage, the prophet Isaiah tells the people of God, "For your light has come! And the glory of the Lord is risen upon you" (v. 1).

What is it then that will be included in the "all things" that will be restored? It is the Body of Christ, the family of God. He (Christ) is restoring the house, the dwelling place of the Lord, that He might come to that house and fill it with His glory.

His house is not made of brick or stone, but of "living stones" being built into a spiritual house (1 Pet. 2:5). His house consists of men and women, flesh and blood, hearts made one with His. We are His Body, His dwelling place. We are the image bearers on earth of almighty God.

From the beginning, He made known His intent:

> So God created man[kind] in His own image; in the image of God He created him; male and female He created them. Then God blessed them, and God said to them, "Be fruitful and multiply; fill the earth and subdue it; have dominion over the fish of the sea, over the birds of the air, and over every living thing that moves on the earth" (Gen. 1:27,28).

The man and woman were the beginning place, the foundation of the House of the Lord—the place where He would dwell and begin to reveal Himself on earth. Through them, God intended to accomplish something for Himself on earth that would ultimately speak, not only from generation to generation, but also on into eternity, into the ages to come.

He specifically fashioned this union, this relationship, to vividly and accurately display His image, His heart, His character on earth.

God's plan was not a secret. It had been publicly declared to the universe and God's archenemy had heard it. The enemy knew that the plan's success depended on the unity and trust of these two people, for together they bore God's image.

Once again Satan endeavored to rise up against God, to exalt his throne, his rule, above the throne of God and he knew right where to strike (see Isa. 14:13,14). He knew it was essential to bring separation, distrust, fear and suspicion between male and female, the image bearers God purposed to use for His unfolding plan on earth. The strength of the man and woman was in their union. Without unity, without oneness, God's plan would fail.

Satan struck and his strategy worked. In shame, blame and distrust, Adam and Eve covered themselves from each other even before they hid from God. God's original design was broken, His image corrupted. We know that the human race continues to suffer the fallout from Satan's malignant coup, but the sad truth is that the Church itself has not fully recovered from this catastrophic event. We in the Body of Christ have yet to experience a very key and vital element of reconciliation: that between man and woman. This relationship, above all others, is the foundational place from which God will work to accomplish His ultimate intention.

Today, the Holy Spirit is working to open our eyes so that we might open our hearts to one another. He is bringing restoration to this first relationship between man and woman—the image bearers of God.

In all expressions of reconciliation, not only must our eyes be opened to see how we have wounded one another, but our hearts must also be humbled and broken before God for the ways we have allowed ourselves to be used by the enemy to further his insidious plan. Through our repentance, we will discover that we have ignorantly contributed to the delay of the very thing we have longed for the most— the full expression of God's kingdom on earth.

Through the man and woman together, God is fully revealed. The restoration of that relationship will again return us to the place of abundant blessing and purpose God revealed at the beginning of time.

In *The House of the Lord*, Francis Frangipane says, "If we will gain God's greatest blessings we must embrace His highest purpose."[2]

My prayer is that this book will be a tool in the hand of God to help return us to His highest purpose.

The Father and His Family

—⚊—

He also has planted eternity in men's hearts and
minds [a divinely implanted sense of a purpose
working through the ages which nothing under
the sun but God alone can satisfy].

ECCLESIASTES 3:11 (AMP.)

In the spring of 1994, the bird romance first hit the front page of our local newspaper. Love was literally "in the air" as a pair of peregrine falcons courted high above the streets of the downtown area. Daily these two birds cavorted in the skies, diving past office windows and weaving in and out among the tall buildings. Ultimately, their love blossomed in the airy heights and they built a "home" on the ledge of the fifty-sixth floor of the Washington Mutual Tower.

Dubbed Stewart and Virginia, after the intersection beneath them, the two falcons settled in to have a family atop one of the skyscrapers. The falcons soon became the topic of conversation in the Puget Sound area, particularly after Virginia laid several eggs.

Television cameras arrived on location and zoomed in on this little family-in-the-making, providing local viewers with nightly updates. One of the banks installed a monitor so customers doing their banking could watch their progress. "Have you heard anything new about the falcons?" "Is their nest still intact?" "Have the eggs hatched yet?" Everyone, it seemed, wanted to chat about the birds.

For three months, the fascinated citizens of Seattle focused on the falcon family, daily searching the skies for every new development. Pedestrians on the street below and office workers high up in the surrounding buildings kept close track of the birds.

Finally the eggs hatched and Virginia and Stewart welcomed three falcon babies. A family was born and the whole city cheered.

Then, abruptly, tragedy struck.

While out on a food-gathering mission, Virginia became confused by the reflections in the high-rise windows, and crashed headlong against the side of the building. Her lifeless body plummeted to the sidewalk below and her death signaled the breakup of the family.

—∞—

Much more was happening here than mere curiosity about some falcons. The relationship observed in the bird family had struck a responsive chord in human hearts: This is the way life is supposed to be.

—∞—

Without their mother, the week-old babies could not protect themselves from the cold so they were taken from their nest by a local zookeeper and a falcon research expert. Papa Stewart, meanwhile, returned to the ledge only to find his offspring gone.

Reflecting on the Falcons

The falcon saga passed. A quiet sense of loss drifted down upon a city that, for a brief time, had drawn together in a strong bond of affection for a little bird family. Here in the midst of a high-tech, sophisticated metropolis, attorneys in their skyscrapers had left serious legal negotiations to walk by the windows and check in on the falcons. Engineers had taken breaks from their computers to monitor "life on the ledge."

Clerks and secretaries on their noontime breaks had walked under the nest and scanned the skies for falcon activity.

More than once I mentally replayed the stark contrast of the whole event, pondering the impression it made on the collective heart of a fast-paced city. I found it interesting that a little bird family could hold such a powerful fascination for so many people, that they empathized so closely with the courtship, marriage and births of a bird family.

Here in Seattle, for those few short months, a city full of broken people—people who struggle and fail in relationships—watched a little bird family and cheered as the family came together and seemed to flourish, then mourned as the family fell apart.

Much more was happening here than mere curiosity about some falcons. The relationship observed in the bird family had struck a responsive chord in human hearts: This is the way life is supposed to be. This is how life was really designed to work. It was a real-life demonstration that "God's invisible qualities—his eternal power and divine nature—have been clearly seen [in creation]" (Rom. 1:20, *NIV*). In other words, God's heart—what He wants and desires for His people—is reflected in the created world for all to see. No wonder we were so touched by the bird scenario. The drama played out high above the ground clearly showed us that family, relationship and intimacy are on the Father's heart.

A broken society filled with broken people—men and women who flounder in their marriages, struggle in relationships, leave behind families in brokenness and sorrow only to move on to start another— still inwardly responds to the real "stuff" of a family, even when demonstrated by birds. Love, belonging, unity, warmth and safety are all the dynamics of a family as God intended it to be. The falcon family was like a neon sign, high in the sky, blinking out a clear and unchanging message: *Family was God's idea, and it is good!*

Family—An Outflow of the Father's Heart

Many voices are telling us that the concept of family is outmoded, even unrealistic in today's society. We see families all around us shattering and experiencing devastation at an alarming rate. We hear the clamoring of increased demands in the gay community for same-sex marriages, live-in lovers insisting that "marriage is just a piece of paper."

Added to that, the radical feminists are declaring, "We don't need men, we can do it on our own!"

From the beginning, family was the centerpiece of God's creation. When God created the heavens and the earth, He didn't just reach "out there somewhere" to arbitrarily devise a plan for this new creation. Because He is omnipotent (all-powerful) and omniscient (all-knowing), He could have designed the earth and its inhabitants to function any way He chose.

God, however, is first of all a Father. This is His initial, most fundamental identity. We see Him reveal Himself in this role at the beginning of Creation and time as we know it today. Knowing God as Father, author DeVern Fromke states, "solves the enigma of life and purpose."

In his book *The Ultimate Intention*, he declares that from this perspective,

> Suddenly we recognize why the Apostle Paul always started back in the heart of the eternal Father before the foundation of the world. Paul always started with God's vital (self-sharing) Fatherhood. It was not with the Father's varied activities, nor with His wondrous attributes that Paul started; it was with the Person, who He chiefly is: THE FATHER. Thus *God's vital Fatherhood* is seen to be the controlling and ultimate factor which determines all His activities. Everything takes on full meaning when it has a *paternal eternal coloring*. We understand why He has done all He has. New light breaks on the future. What would a Father desire, purpose and ultimately intend?[1] (Emphasis added.)

God put us in families as an outflow of His own "Father-heart."

After His Likeness

Because God is a Father, has the nature of a Father and is alone the source of all goodness, He wanted to reproduce Himself and fill the earth with His own image—all that He is. All of His characteristics—His love, His gentleness, His mercy, His grace—were attributes of a Father for His children, attributes that He intended to reproduce in them. He wanted all of creation, especially "the principalities and powers in heavenly places," to be able to look at His family and His children and recognize that God was indeed their Father. In them, the beauty of His Father-heart and nature would be displayed (see Eph. 3:9-11).

This gives greater meaning to the words we read in Genesis 1:26 when God said, "Let Us make man in Our image, according to Our likeness" (that they might bear the stamp of our likeness). Humanity was meant to bear more than a rational or moral likeness to God.[2] He intended that His own Spirit be placed within us. A. W. Tozer agrees:

> Deep inside every human being there is a private sanctum, a sacred place where only God can dwell. He has planted something of Himself (eternity) in every human breast...a divinely implanted sense of purpose which nothing or no one but God can satisfy. This place is called the spirit of a man. And that which makes him a human being is not his body but his spirit, the place in which the image of God was made to rest.[3]

The heart, or spirit, of each human being is where God desired to dwell, where He would reveal Himself to bring growth and change in our lives. God reproduces His likeness in the heart.

"Father," a Relational Term

God not only wanted to reproduce Himself and fill the earth with His likeness, He also longed for a family. "Father" is a relational term. God wanted children with whom He could share His life. He wanted a people who would love and respond to Him, a people who would have the capacity to know Him and have intimate fellowship with Him.

As a further expression of being created in His image as "Father," God would gift humanity—male and female together—with the privilege of expanding His family.

From before the foundation of the world, family was God's design for men and women. Family was a place where they could belong, know love, be affirmed and experience intimacy. It was a place where their children would receive a name and an identity, all as an expression of His heart for His own family. Paul declares that "from whom [the Father] every [the whole] family in heaven and on earth derives its name [character, nature]" (Eph. 3:15, *NASB*).[4]

As an all-wise Father, God knew how life would work best for us, and He designed it all accordingly.

The Family Line

The framework of family, then, issued from the Father's heart. It was set in place from the beginning, and has held a significant, ongoing place of purpose down through history.

God began His family with one man, Adam, created in His own image, but soon declared that Adam's solitary condition was "not good." In response to this problem, the woman was brought forth out of the man and at this point, "God blessed them, and God said to them,

—⚭—

The kingdom of God—the nature and character of God, as well as the outworking of God's plan on earth—was to be played out in and through man and woman and the concept of family. There God pronounces His blessing.

—⚭—

'Be fruitful and multiply'" (Gen. 1:28). In other words, *they were to become a family.*

The kingdom of God—the nature and character of God, as well as the outworking of God's plan on earth—was to be played out in and through man and woman and the concept of family. There God pronounces His blessing.

This emphasis continues in Genesis 9:1, following the devastation of the flood. God again underscores the concept and structure of the family as He blesses Noah, telling him he also was to be fruitful and multiply—and become a family.

In Genesis 12, Abram's blessing from God states, "In you all the families of the earth shall be blessed" (v. 3).

When the men were circumcised as a sign of the covenant in Genesis 17, it was done according to families.

Biblical genealogies, listing families, were of utmost importance in God's record keeping.

In Exodus 12:3 we read about the advent of Passover. The Israelites were instructed to "take a lamb for themselves, *according to their fathers' households,* a lamb for *each household*" (*NASB,* italics added).

The Israelite tribes were positioned around the tabernacle "according to their father's houses" (Num. 2:34).

Nehemiah, when overseeing the restoration of the wall around Jerusalem, stationed the people to work in front of their own houses "according to their families" (Neh. 4:13).

In Hebrews 3:6, the followers of Christ are called the household or family of God. The Church is the fulfillment of God's plan to have a family for Himself. Here, no one is left out. The broken, the hurting, the widow and the orphans all have a place. Singles are included. The psalmist's words reflect God's tender provision for those alone: "God sets the solitary in families" (Ps. 68:6); "[He is] a father of the fatherless, a defender of widows" (v. 5).

The pattern is plain. Yet one event is so profound in its implication that everything we have said to this point pales by comparison. The greatest revelation of the heart of God regarding family came in the person of His Son, Jesus—the One who came to earth to reveal the Father to us. Jesus was the embodiment of the way, the truth and the life. Yet He was born into a humble family. He was raised by a mother and a father. He had siblings. He lived for 30 years in a home, with a family, before He ever taught or performed a miracle. At age 12, He came to the Temple and spoke with such authority that the teachers of the law were confounded. The wisdom of this young boy was amazing.

Jesus, as He was in the Temple, grasped what it meant to be in His Father's house and longed to be about His Father's business. Yet He returned to His own home, humbly submitting Himself to parental guidance. In this family setting, the boy grew "in wisdom and stature, and in favor with God and men" (Luke 2:52).

Clearly, then, we see that the family is God's design. It was His choice and plan. He gave it His highest endorsement when He placed His own Son within its protective, nurturing walls. Within this framework, His plan for humanity and for Himself will best come to fulfillment. In the context of family, we experience the sense of belonging and bonding for which our hearts long. Here we receive not only the love and nurturing

—∞—

In the context of family, we experience the sense of belonging and bonding for which our hearts long.

—∞—

we need, but also the opportunity for maturing and growth that brings forth sons and daughters in the image of their Father God in a healthy way. In this environment we too "grow in wisdom and stature, and in favor with God and men."

The Big Breakdown

When the backbone of God's framework crumbles, all of life is thrown out of joint. Pain, disintegration, dysfunction and brokenness will be the excruciating result. We don't have to look beyond our own cities and neighborhoods to realize that this is a description of our world today. As family life continues to splinter, society as a whole suffers.

According to David Blankenhorn, author of *Fatherless America*, "[Forty] percent of American children will go to sleep tonight in homes in which their fathers do not live." He goes on to say, "The most urgent social problem in America today is fatherlessness. Fatherlessness is the most harmful demographic trend in this generation. It is the leading cause of declining child well-being in our society and is the engine driving our most urgent social problems from crime to adolescent pregnancy to child sexual abuse to domestic violence against women."[5]

Looking Elsewhere

"If we don't have a family, we'll find one." The needs of the bruised and broken victims of family breakdowns cry out for fulfillment. Many of these hurting people who chose to leave their own families ultimately seek out a substitute "family."

I think of the 1960s as a time when young people by the thousands were casting aside restraint and "living free." For many of them, leaving home seemed like the "freest" way to live.

Yet, on the heels of their rejection of family constraints, they joined groups demanding even greater constraints, such as the Hare Krishnas, Moonies and other religious cults. Meditating together became the "in" thing. Others connected with groupies who did drugs together, or became part of the "street scene." Like the prodigal son, they were running from family, but were quick to replace it with another. In their hearts, like everyone, they wanted to "belong," to be part of something greater than themselves. Their identity and security, they were learning, could not be found in individualism.

Today, teenage gangs, another kind of "family," are on the rise around the world. In the United States, they are the source of the most serious increase in the number of violent crimes committed across the nation. In Rio de Janeiro the need to belong, to be cared for, is so strong for the thousands of street children, they instinctively band together, forming "families" in the midst of their homelessness.

The sense of structure and belonging these alternative groups offer often comes with a shattering price tag. Such things as mind control, brainwashing, drug activity, physical and sexual abuse can all be integral parts of these communities. The cost to individual lives and society in general has been incalculable.

The saddest aspect of all, however, is that any system not based on God's design will ultimately fall desperately short in the ability to provide the true intimacy for which we were created.

Only God Can Set Things Right

In a recent sermon one of my pastor friends, Mike McIntosh of Grace Church in Federal Way, Washington, made some defining observations about the nature and purpose of families:

So often we hear that the world is too intense, too violent,

too ugly, and that's what is destroying our homes. It is not
the world that is destroying our homes. It is the weakness
of our homes that is destroying our world.

Pastor McIntosh goes on to point out, "The harvest springs from the
seed, the seed doesn't spring from the harvest." In asserting this
sequence, he underscores a strong point: God has deposited a powerful
influence in families. If these small societal units are strong and healthy,
they will influence the larger world around them with their strength.
Stable homes produce stable societies, not the other way around.

"The strength of a nation," McIntosh emphasizes, "is the strength of
its families. It is not a strong nation that makes families safe. It is the
strong families that make a nation prosperous. The family is both a
refuge and a launching point for change in society."

Pastor McIntosh is right. The health of society depends on the
health of families. Greater still is the health of God's family, His house,
the dwelling place of His Spirit. God's own family has been devastated
and fragmented. Alienation, divorce and family breakdown have been
as rampant within the Church as without.

God's Word tells us that the place where He will begin to "set things
in right order" will be His house, for here He intends to demonstrate His
heart and nature to the world: "For the time has come for judgment to
begin at the house of God" (1 Pet. 4:17). His house is where restoration
will begin. Here we will begin to see His glorious purposes unfold in
ever-increasing ways as we move toward the end of this age called time.

As stated in our introduction, God's plan was not a secret. It was
spoken out clearly on earth. God would have a family in His likeness
that would represent Him in the earth and thus rule in His name
(nature). Satan heard, and launched his attack at the heart of the plan.
To render this plan of God ineffective, he must target the foundation—
of society, of the Church, of God's family—the man and woman.
"Divide and conquer" has been an effective tactic of many a war strate-
gist, a tactic of which Satan is a master. United we stand, divided we
fall. We know that God's blessing was upon this union, that "there [in
unity] the Lord commanded the blessing" (Ps. 133:3).

God is moving by His Holy Spirit in a strategic way. The reconciliation movement that has begun between races and denominations is a

foretaste of even greater things to come. God is wanting to go further and heal the rupture within each race, within each denomination—the division between male and female, the first relationship—not only in individual couples, but in the corporate Church as well.

Only God can reveal to us the degree to which the enemy has wrought his devastation, the loss of strength and power the Church has suffered because of this alienation. Yet with great joy I have come to announce, "Good news is on the horizon!"

—*⚂*—

Something to Think About

- What did we discover was God's most basic and fundamental nature?
- What was the sign of God's crowning endorsement of family? Does this fact affect your viewpoint of family? How?
- What does Psalm 133 tell us will be the result of unity? What then is the result of disunity?

- 2 -

Restoration

—⚬⚬—

For the time being he must remain out of sight in
heaven until everything is restored to order again
just the way God, through the preaching of his
holy prophets of old, said it would be.

ACTS 3:21 *(THE MESSAGE)*

Restoration! The very sound of the word exhilarates me. It stirs my love of decorating. I love to take something that is old or broken and restore it to life. Often, to my delight, that same piece becomes the focal point of a room, adding its charm and newfound life in a way that enhances everything around it.

I remember a few years ago needing to "work my magic" on an entire room—our master bedroom. I made several attempts to give this room the special touch it needed, but finally realized it just was not coming together the way I had hoped.

In complete frustration I called my friend Bette, a professional interior designer. "Help!" I pleaded. "I need your expert opinion!" I'll never forget the day she arrived at my home, her arms loaded with books, large rings holding swatches of material, paint chips and carpet samples galore. How would I ever be able to make a choice out of all this? As we made our way upstairs, Bette assured me she would assist and guide me through the whole process of restoration until the work was accomplished.

Bette began her gentle probing: "What do you like? What do you hope this room will look and feel like when we're done?"

I had to think of color combinations. Was it to be a traditional room, or would I prefer a more sleek, contemporary look? Did I want to blend some of my present things with the new that was to be added?

As I shared my heart, Bette listened, gathering pertinent information that would enable her to discern just what direction we should head. The selected carpet sample was grouped with the swatch of material that would one day make up our bedspread, drapes and pillows. Placed alongside was a picture she had drawn to show the placement of furniture and other accent pieces.

We moved back to look at our selection. Suddenly, Bette, in her typical effusive manner, threw her arms in the air and exclaimed, "Oh, isn't it just beautiful!" Turning to meet my startled expression she quickly added, "When I get a room this far, to me it's as good as finished!"

I couldn't help but think how like God that is. Here we were, standing in an old, unrestored room, stains on the carpet, walls badly needing fresh paint, and worn furniture that needed to be replaced. At this point the old was all I could see, save a few scraps of material and the promise of an expert to restore my room.

Yet to the expert it was as good as finished! She had confidence in her ability—her expertise—to bring about just what was needed. She had done it time and again. The scenario had been repeated from home to home: Restore the old and bring forth the new, just as God has done in individuals and families again and again through the centuries.

Yet there is a larger truth here. God, the Master Builder Himself, saw His works finished before they were begun. Hebrews 4:3 tells us, "[His] works were finished from the foundation [the conception or beginning][1] of the world." From the moment God conceived in His mind to create a family for Himself—before the first stars of humanity's earthly home were hung in the sky, knowing all it would cost Him—His plan was finished. God knew that the beauty of His creation would become corrupted, that sin and death would enter in, that hearts would become stained and marred, needing to be replaced with new ones.

Yet He went ahead with His plan because He knew He could fix it.

Indeed, God did not begin His work of creation until everything that was needed to bring His children to their ultimate destination—that of being changed into His image, living in eternal, unbroken fellowship

—⚊⚊—

Restoration is not just something on the heart of God; it is the heart of God!

—⚊⚊—

with Himself, fulfilling all that we were created to be and do—was guaranteed and in place. Jesus, before He ever arrived on the scene, was the guarantee, the covenant Lamb, "slain from the foundation of the world" (Rev. 13:8).

God's Heart

As "a faithful Creator" (1 Pet. 4:19), God covenanted to restore us even before He created us. Restoration is not just something on the heart of God; it is the heart of God! It is inextricable from His nature. As such, it is a theme that runs throughout Scripture: "I have torn but I will heal...I have smitten but I will bind up...I have pulled down but I will plant again...I have scattered but I will gather them...I will fetch them...I will bring them again" (see Jer. 31:10; Hos. 6:1).

Restoration is the reason Jesus came to earth. He came not only to redeem us from the fall—to buy us back from death and hell—as essential and wonderful as that was. In great reverence, I say that redemption was just the first step in God's ultimate plan for us. It was, as DeVern Fromke says in *The Ultimate Intention*, "a parentheses incorporated into the main theme. Redemption was not the end but only a recovery program,"[2] incorporated to return us to God's larger purposes, which He planned from the beginning.

Luke's Gospel opens by telling us, "[He] has raised up a horn of salvation for us" (1:69). "Salvation" is an all-inclusive term. It means "to deliver, protect, heal, preserve, make whole."[3] In other words, "restore."

Consider Webster's definition of "restore": "to bring back to a former or normal condition by repairing, rebuilding, altering, to bring back to health and strength, to put back in a position or rank."

God's purpose in sending Jesus was that we would receive restoration in every dimension of our lives: body, soul, spirit and purpose. "He has borne our griefs [sicknesses] and carried [away] our sorrows;…He was wounded for our transgressions, He was bruised for our iniquities; the chastisement for our peace was upon Him, and by His stripes we are healed" (Isa. 53:4,5). "[God] raised us up together, and made us sit together in the heavenly places in Christ Jesus" (Eph. 2:6).

God wants to make us whole; that's why Jesus suffered and died! Jesus, the Creator of the universe, died to restore that which He created; and He bore more than just our sins. He suffered death that we might experience peace, healing and a sense of purpose or destiny, all of which are necessary for wholeness. Restoration is at the heart of the gospel because it expresses the very heart of the Father.

Corporate Headquarters

God's plan for redemption and restoration is not only individual, but it is also corporate. His intention has always been to build His children together into a corporate house for Himself. He wanted to fit us together in Christ that we might grow "into a holy temple in the Lord, in whom you also are being built together for a dwelling place of God in the Spirit" (Eph 2:21,22). This meant male and female, black and white, all of us who are called by His name.

When Scripture states that the heavens will retain Him until all things have been restored, it is telling us that Jesus will not return for a Body that is still divided, weak and broken, a Body of people who blindly walk in darkness, oblivious to God's plan and purpose for them. He will not skip over or ignore the many prophetic promises of restoration He has spoken of to His people from the beginning of time. "For truly I tell you, until the sky and earth pass away and perish, not one smallest letter nor one little hook [identifying certain Hebrew letters] will pass from the Law until all things [it foreshadows] are accomplished" (Matt. 5:18, *Amp.*).

God will bring us back to what He purposed for us from before the time of the Fall. His family, His Body, His kingdom will yet be seen as the glorious expression of His life, just as He has spoken. He will yet fill His house with His presence and glory. He will display to the world what He purposed for us as men and women from the beginning. He will reveal His way, His truth and His life through us as we become restored once again to His glorious design.

An Unprecedented Move

Restoration has begun! In the past 30 years, we have witnessed an unprecedented move of God. The late 1960s signaled a sweeping move of God's Spirit that touched both men and women, but what has taken place in the lives of women in this time has been especially unique and unusual.

If we look back in history, we can see that God has always used women. Many times God's ongoing plan seemed to hinge on the response of a woman. As we read through Scripture, however, it appears that when God worked through women, He worked primarily through individual women—a Jochabed here, a Deborah or an Esther there. Never in all of history has there been the kind of corporate calling forth or worldwide awakening of women such as we have seen in the past 30 years.

Aglow International and other women's ministries were birthed during this time in response to the massive heart cry of women to know more of God. My association with Aglow since the earliest days of the ministry has given me an experiential view of what God has been doing in the hearts of women on many fronts around the world. When Aglow began in 1967 in the Seattle area, there were no grandiose thoughts of it becoming worldwide in scope, no awareness that this was, in fact, the emergence of a move of God's Spirit that would touch the women of the world in such an ongoing and purposeful way. Yet growth, extension and expansion soon began to take place. God, it seemed, was up to something on earth that had to do specifically with women. Groups started to meet across the United States. Soon women from other nations were contacting the Aglow leaders, wanting to know how to begin chapters in their areas as well. Today Aglow is ministering in more than 70 percent of the world's nations.

What was God up to? What was the purpose of this unprecedented move that seemed to single out women in such an undeniably specific way? The question was too obvious to ignore. As the Word states in Amos 3:7, "Surely the Lord God does nothing, unless He reveals His secret to His servants the prophets."

—⬩⬩⬩—

God is not reluctant to make His will known to His people. He is always wanting to reveal His heart and plan to us so that we might walk with Him according to understanding, and to be able to cooperate with Him in it.

—⬩⬩⬩—

In other words, God is not reluctant to make His will known to His people. He is always wanting to reveal His heart and plan to us so that we might walk with Him according to understanding, and to be able to cooperate with Him in it.

All Means All

Ephesians 1:11 tells us, "[He] works all things according to the counsel of His will." *All* things! Not just a few things, not even several things, but all things. All means everything, every bit, every part, everyone. It is all inclusive. He overlooks nothing. We understand that God has a plan to be fulfilled on earth, and this verse tells us that everything God does He does keeping in mind the fulfillment of that plan. He does not waste time or motion. Everything He does has purpose and significance. We may not always understand the events that are taking place in our lives, but one thing we can know is that God, as Master Builder, is always at work bringing about His master plan for us. Not just for our sake, but for His own.

The unprecedented move of God's Spirit in the lives of women fits into this category. It is one of the "all things" God is working after the council of His will. God is up to something and we need to discern what it is. Why would it be so important or significant for Him to orchestrate a global awakening among women? To what are women being awakened? I believe a final, critical restoration has begun.

God's Representative

Because the heavens will retain Jesus until all things have been restored, we can be sure He wants us to understand what the nature of that restoration will be. To know what God is about, to properly discern what He originally planned for His creation, we have to go back to the beginning and follow the order of events as God has given them to us there.

As the door of time opens, we hear God saying these words:

> "Let Us make man in Our image, according to Our likeness";...So God created man in His own image; in the image of God He created him; male and female He created them. Then God blessed them, and God said to them, "Be fruitful and multiply; fill the earth and subdue it; have dominion over the fish of the sea, over the birds of the air, and over every living thing that moves on the earth" (Gen. 1:26-28).

God was speaking His purpose for humanity. First, He stated that humans would be made in the image of God. "Image," according to *Strong's*, means "representative figure." To say that humans are made in God's "image" means "that man is like God and that man represents God."[4] As such, Adam was to represent God on earth and be the expression of His wonderful life to the world around him, beginning in the Garden of Eden. Adam was to be the beginning of a people who would be linked to God in a life-giving, life-sharing union. He was to walk in authority, taking dominion over the earth and over anything that would counter the rule and plan of God.

God made very clear just what "taking dominion" meant for Adam. As we will see, He also offered him the much-needed strength and power for the task that would enable him to "stand" for God on earth.

Adam and Eve were first told to "be fruitful and multiply." Let's look at what these words mean:

- Fruitful: to bear or bring forth fruit, to grow, to increase.
- Multiply: to increase (in whatever respect), to bring up, enlarge, grow up.[5]

God wanted His people to increase, not only physically, but also spiritually, and thereby to be in authority. They were to mature into a mighty power that would effectively overcome any enemy they might face. Pharaoh (analogous to Satan in Scripture) expressed his fear of this very thing when he said in Exodus 1:10,11, "Let us deal shrewdly with them [the Hebrew nation], lest they multiply, and it happen, in the event of war, that they also join our enemies and fight against us."

In addition to increasing, they were to "subdue and have dominion."

"Subdue" means "to conquer, bring into bondage, tread down, to force, keep under, bring into subjection."[6] Although some might say this merely means Adam and Eve were to subdue the plants and animals, it is much too strong a word to refer to a creation that was, at that point, in harmony with them. This word is used in other places to refer to subduing enemy lands and people.[7]

According to the *Theological Wordbook of the Old Testament*, the Hebrew word *kabash* means "to make to serve, by force if necessary" and "assumes that the party being subdued is hostile to the subduer."[8]

"Dominion" is similar to "subdue" and is defined as "[to] prevail against, reign or to rule over, tread down or subjugate."[9]

Earlier, according to the second account of Creation in Genesis 2, Adam himself was instructed to "tend and guard" the garden (v. 15, *Amp*.).

In this "law of first mention" (the first place something is mentioned in Scripture, which sets the groundwork for all further references to that same subject), we see clearly that humanity was made for authority. This was the job description given to God's first image bearers: initially the man, and subsequently the man and woman together. From the moment of Adam's creation, a force was already loose in the earth against which Adam was instructed to guard and protect his sanctuary. Ultimately, Adam and Eve together were commissioned to subdue and be in authority over all the earth.

The enemy they were to subdue was God's enemy—Satan—the one who had attempted to exalt himself and "be like the Most High" (Isa. 14:14). Already he was prowling the earth looking for someone to devour, outraged at any intention of God to subdue him through mere humans. After all, as we see in Ezekiel 28:14, he had been "the anointed cherub who covers," indicating high office and having authority and responsibility to protect and defend the holy mountain of God.[10] He was the seal of perfection, full of wisdom and perfect in beauty. He was perfect in his ways until iniquity was found in him. He was lifted up because of his beauty, he corrupted his wisdom, and was therefore cast out of the mountain of God (see vv. 12-19).

From the time Lucifer rose up against God declaring his intent to exalt himself above God, God's response was swift and very direct:

> Your pomp is brought down to Sheol,....How you are fallen from heaven, O Lucifer, son of the morning! How you are cut down to the ground, you who weakened the nations! Yet you shall be brought down to Sheol, to the lowest depths of the Pit. Those who see you will gaze at you, and consider you, saying: "Is this the man who made the earth tremble, who shook kingdoms, who made the world as a wilderness and destroyed its cities, who did not open the house of his prisoners?" The Lord of hosts has sworn, saying, "Surely, as I have thought, so it shall come to pass, and as I have purposed, so it shall stand: that I will break the Assyrian [a type of anti-Christ spirit] in My land, and on My mountains tread him underfoot....This is the purpose that is purposed against the whole earth, and this is the hand that is stretched out over all the nations. For the Lord of hosts has purposed, and who will annul it? His hand is stretched out, and who will turn it back?" (Isa. 14:11,12,15-17,24-27).

God had declared war on His enemy! Satan was to be brought down to the pit of Sheol—he would be trodden underfoot. The eyes of God's people were to be opened to who he really is: the one who made the world a wilderness and brought destruction to its cities. In this event God would be supremely glorified. In His infinite wisdom, God would use mere humans—weak, frail, puny flesh—to subdue the one (Satan) who had officiated in the heavenly realms. What an insult!

An Earthly Schoolroom

In the meantime, God had some lessons He wanted to teach. Donald Barnhouse, in his book *The Invisible War*, describes it this way:

> The great governing cherub had become the malignant enemy. Our God was neither surprised nor astonished, for, of course, He knew before it happened that it would happen, and He had His perfect plan ready to be put into effect. Although the Lord had the power to destroy Satan with a breath, He did not do so. It was as though an edict had been proclaimed in heaven: We shall give this rebellion a thorough trial. We shall permit it to run its full course. The universe shall see what a creature, though he be the highest creature ever to spring from God's word, can do apart from Him. We shall watch this experiment, and permit the universe of creatures to watch it, during this brief interlude called time. In it the spirit of independence shall be allowed to expand to the utmost. And the wreck and ruin which shall result will demonstrate to the universe, and forever, that there is no life, no joy, no peace apart from a complete dependence upon the Most High God, Possessor of Heaven and Earth.[11]

The earth had been made for humanity to rule over on God's behalf, but dominion would not come without a conflict. David understood this and spoke of it in Psalm 8:

> Out of the mouth of babes and nursing infants You have ordained strength, because of Your enemies, that You may silence the enemy and the avenger. You have made him [humans] to have dominion over the works of Your hands; You have put all things under his feet (vv. 2,6).

God intended that the process of learning to take dominion over the works of His hands would have a twofold purpose for Adam and Eve and their resulting progeny. First, they would grow up into maturity, not only physically and mentally, but also spiritually. Second, they would learn to know their God and become "sons" (and daughters) in the fullest and most intimate sense of the word.

The enigma in all this was that the task was too great for them. They were outclassed; the enemy they were to conquer was too strong. God knew it and He deliberately orchestrated it. This impossible situation was to be the "schoolroom" of their learning.

—*ᘯ*—

Something to Think About

- Reread Revelation 13:8. What did God do to ensure that all He planned for humanity would come to pass?
- "Image" is a key word that tells us God's plan and purpose for His family. What does "image" as used in the creation story mean? What does it mean to you?
- Another key word that tells what one of humanity's most significant duties would be is "subdue." What does the word mean, and to whom does it apply?

- 3 -

A Tale of Two Trees

—♒—

The tree of life was also in the midst

of the garden, and the tree of the

knowledge of good and evil.

GENESIS 2:9

"What were some of the consequences of the Fall of humanity?" queried the teacher from the front of the adult Sunday School class.

"Work!" several quickly responded while others groaned in agreement.

This seems to be a common perception among Christians. In the midst of our exhausted, frenzied lives, many of us are sure that what made the Garden of Eden "paradise" for Adam and Eve was that they did not have to work. Their days would have consisted of leisurely walks in the sun, naps in a hammock and popping grapes for entertainment. In a world filled with frantic activity, fighting commuter traffic, racing to meet deadlines and other people's schedules, that idea can sound deliciously inviting to us—for a while.

A life of leisure, however, was not God's plan for Adam and Eve. Far from it! Nor was frenzy, worry and fear—anxiously earning their bread by the sweat of their brow—His first plan for them. God's design was work to accomplish His purposes on earth, and work founded in rest and security based on the sure provision of God's blessing and power.

It was a work of great magnitude, and it would not be accomplished without resistance. Satan was indeed a malignant enemy, but God intended nothing short of full victory.

We see that God begins to make known His plan for Adam in Genesis 2:15, before the woman is brought onto the scene. Here we are told, "[God]...put him into the garden of Eden to dress it and to keep it" *(KJV).* To fully understand what God was about, we need to look carefully at these words. In a surface reading, the two words "dress" and "keep" seem rather innocuous and almost a repeat of each other. Not so.

"Dress" means to "tend or till," literally "to work,"[1] but the word "keep" catches our attention. It means "to hedge about, i.e., to guard; protect, beware, be circumspect, observe, preserve, watch (-man)."[2] Genesis 3:24 uses the same word to tell us that the cherubim and the flaming sword were placed at the east of the Garden of Eden after the Fall "to keep" *(KJV)* and "guard" the way of the tree of life so that no one could approach it.

Here again we have a word that tells us that an enemy was already lying in wait. Adam was to guard the garden, actually to be a watchman over it against any hostile intrusion. This work was far too much for mere humans. God knew it (and so did Satan). Immediately following His command to Adam to watch over and protect the garden, God tells him what he will need for the job:

> And out of the ground the Lord God made every tree grow that is pleasant to the sight and good for food. The tree of life was also in the midst of the garden, and the tree of the knowledge of good and evil. And the Lord God command-ed the man, saying, "Of every tree of the garden you may freely eat; but of the tree of the knowledge of good and evil you shall not eat, for in the day that you eat of it you shall surely die" (Gen. 2:9,16,17).

God's Provision

When God placed Adam in the garden, telling him to guard and pro-tect it, God did not intend that Adam should do so in his own strength. From the inception of God's plan, provision had been made, and the provision was none other than the tree of life, representative of imparting the life of God to this new creature. If Adam was to reign and rule as planned—if he was to have the ability to stand against, to be in authority over God's enemy, Satan—then he would indeed need something far beyond his own puny strength. Therefore, God not only provided Adam with the physical food of herbs and other trees, but spiritual food as well—His own life—the tree of life.

Adam was commanded to partake of it; it was not a suggestion. It was a command because it was a necessity. His life depended on it. The future of God's plan depended on it. Authority over the enemy depended on it. Therefore, God uses strong language here and commands, urges, the man to partake. As Watchman Nee so beautifully states in his book *The Messenger of the Cross*:

> Of all the edible trees, this one [the tree of life] is the most important. This is what Adam should have eaten first. Why is this so? The tree of life signifies the life of God, the uncreated life of God. Adam is a created being, and therefore he does not possess such uncreated life. Though at this point he is still without sin, he nevertheless is only natural since he has not received the holy life of God. The purpose of God is for Adam to choose the fruit of the tree of life with his own volition so that he might be related to God in divine life. And thus Adam would move from simply being created by God to his being born of Him as well. What God requires of Adam is simply for him to deny his created, natural life and be joined to Him in divine life, thus living daily by the life of God. Such is the meaning of the tree of life.[3]

DeVern Fromke affirms this truth in *The Ultimate Intention* when, under the heading "Something Adam Never Had," he writes these words:

> Since Adam was but a created being, he was by God's intention only to have created life until such time as he might "become" a partaker of divine Life. God could not thrust divine life upon Adam. The tree of life (typical of the life-

giving, eternal Son), grew in the garden, but Adam had not yet discerned its supreme value. Let us realize that even before Adam sinned, he needed a vital birth relationship in order to become a son, according to the Father's plan. Perhaps nothing has so blighted the vision and growth of believers as the false assumption that Adam in his innocence and sinlessness was all that God ever purposed him to be.[4]

—∾∾—

Adam...is being offered God's own life by which to live, a life of trust and dependence upon Him; indeed he is being commanded to partake of it.

—∾∾—

Adam, then, is being offered God's own life by which to live, a life of trust and dependence upon Him; indeed he is being commanded to partake of it. Juxtaposed to this is the tree of knowledge of good and evil, which represents the way of the flesh, independence, relying on his own strength, choosing his own way.

We must not miss the fact that Adam had a positive command from God to obey (eat), before he had a negative command (do not eat). It is easy to miss, and most of us have. The confusion lies in the words "may" and "freely." "May" does not imply "may or may not," and "freely" does not mean "free to do it or not." "Freely" seems to be a holdover from the *King James* translation, which was correct in its time, but we use the term differently today. It is not an independent word, but is part of the Hebrew word for eat, *akal,* which means to "eat, burn up, consume, devour...freely, (plenty), etc."[5]

Adam was to eat a lot (freely, plenty) of the trees God had provided for his sustenance and strength, most specifically the tree of life. Several sources say Genesis 2:16 is literally translated: "And God commanded the man saying, 'of every tree of the garden *eating thou shalt eat.'"*[6] The repetition of the word "eat" implies "superabundance," and intensifies the strength of the command.

Neither the words "may" nor "freely" indicate God was leaving the "if, when, or how much" to eat to Adam's own discretion. Adam, having free will, could choose not to eat of the provision God had made, but it would be in direct disobedience to the command.

The pattern of God's positive command to partake of His provision before He gives His negative command to resist evil is seen throughout the New Testament.

James 4:7 says, "Submit to God," then, "Resist the devil and he will flee from you." In Ephesians 6:10,11, Paul encourages the believers to "be strong in the Lord and in the power of His might. Put on the whole armor of God, that you may be able to stand against the wiles of the devil." To the Galatians Paul wrote, "Walk in the Spirit, and you shall not fulfill the lust of the flesh" (Gal. 5:16).

This twofold process was clearly evident in Jesus' life. Though conceived by the Holy Spirit, He later received a second impartation of the life of God when the Holy Spirit came upon Him at baptism in the Jordan. Now "being filled with the Holy Spirit," He was immediately led into the wilderness for 40 days, "being tempted...by the devil." Subsequently, empowered by the Spirit in a new way, He began His earthly ministry (see Luke 4:1,2,14,15).

This, then, is the order. It was also Adam's order. What was in God's heart as He gave this command to Adam? Was He simply giving arbitrary instructions and waiting to strike Adam down at the first slip? Surely not. Let's think awhile about the Father's heart.

A Panorama of Love

The Bible, from Genesis to Revelation, is an epic love story—God's love story. It begins with a loving Father desiring to share everything He is and everything He has with His created son, Adam. It ends with a Bridegroom courting and wooing a Bride, the Church, into a loving, life-sharing relationship that will endure throughout all eternity.

"For I know the thoughts and plans that I have for you, says the Lord, thoughts and plans for welfare and peace and not for evil, to give you hope in your final outcome" (Jer. 29:11, *Amp.*). God's thoughts and plans for humanity, beginning with Adam, have always been for our welfare, to give us peace, hope and an expectation of good, as the prophet Jeremiah declares.

—⚏—

We can almost feel the urging of this Father-heart in His words to Adam as He speaks about the need to "partake freely" of every tree with the exception of the tree of knowledge of good and evil.

—⚏—

At Adam's inception, we see the Father making every provision for His son. We can almost feel the urging of this Father-heart in His words to Adam as He speaks about the need to "partake freely" of every tree with the exception of the tree of knowledge of good and evil. In essence, God is saying, "Partake of me that you might live; walk in relationship with me that you might know peace and fulfillment."

God knew what the disastrous results would be to Adam and his progeny if he refused to partake. Brokenness. Pain. Loss of peace. No genuine fulfillment. Death, even while living. Perhaps the parable Jesus told of the prodigal most poignantly underscores the heart of the Father longing for relationship with His son, and the potential results of Adam's reluctance.

The young man in this story of the prodigal wanted his inheritance early, before he had learned enough to handle it wisely. He wanted to leave his father's house and seek out a life for himself. In today's world, such a departure from home and a desire for independence is not thought of as unusual. In the context of the time and culture in which this young man lived, however, his actions would have signaled a serious break with tradition. It showed a heartbreaking disregard for relationship with his father and all that his father had provided for him.

Having asked his father for his inheritance, he took the money and traveled to a far country. He wanted to pursue life on his own terms, take things into his own hands. Soon, he had squandered his inheritance and, when every shekel was gone, a severe famine arose in the land. He began to be in want, to experience the results of his own choices. He began to wonder where his next meal would come from. The pigs he tended ate better than he did.

Finally, he came to himself and said, "How many of my father's hired servants have bread enough and to spare, and I perish with hunger! I will arise and go to my father" (Luke 15:17,18). The cost of his independence had been immense. He had left as a rich man. He would return as a poor man.

Yet the next line so reveals the nature of God the Father. As I read it, it struck a deep and familiar cord in my own heart. "When he was still a great way off, his father saw him" (v. 20). As a parent who has also experienced a young son's "going to a far country," I knew how this father felt. I, too, had felt deep concern for the welfare of my boy. I had a love that could not be snuffed out by the overt, hurtful actions of an immature, foolish and rebellious son. I had a daily longing just to embrace him once again. I imagine not a day went by that the prodigal's father did not wait at the window, the door or the gate, watching. He would have been looking to see if today might be the day his son would return. Today might be the day he would live in relationship with his son once again, to experience all the wonderful provision he delighted to lavish upon him.

The father, upon seeing the son yet at a far distance, ran to meet him and fell on his neck in a welcoming embrace. He hugged and kissed the son again and again, saying, "This my son was dead and is alive again" (v. 24). Although the father welcomed him back with much celebration, surely he had grieved about his son's devastating choices and would have saved him from them if he could.

Adam's Response

This was the heart of God, the heart of Adam's Father. He, too, wanted to save his son from devastation. He wanted to lavish not only His love, but also His life and provision on this, His first created. He wanted to further establish him in his sonship—not just a created son with the breath of God in his being, a living soul, but a living spirit with the life of God flowing within him, empowering, enabling, enriching every facet of his life.

As believers in Christ, we understand that we have become "joint heirs" with Him (Rom. 8:17). This is what God purposed from the beginning, that Adam and Eve be joined with Him in life, reign with Him and take dominion over His creation. Adam was slow, though, and seemingly careless toward the provision that would make it all possible—the tree of life. Indeed, Adam's ultimate choice seems to reflect just this attitude as Romans 5:19 declares:

"For just as by one man's disobedience (failing to hear, heedlessness, and carelessness) the many were constituted sinners" (Amp.).

To this, Vine's An Expository Dictionary of New Testament Words attests, "Carelessness in attitude is the precursor (forerunner) of actual disobedience."[7]

Jesus, the "second Man," (1 Cor. 15:47) who accomplished what the first man failed to do, said of His own life and ministry, "The Son can do nothing of Himself, but what He sees the Father do" (John 5:19). "The Father who dwells in Me does the works" (14:10). "I do not seek My own will but the will of the Father who sent Me" (5:30).

Jesus, the Son of God, who came to earth to live as the pattern Man, knew that He must not live out of His own human resources. He knew that to do the Father's will, He must live by the Father's life and not His own. God purposed no less than that for Adam, but it appears he had not yet learned that "the flesh [even if it was as perfect as Jesus' was] profits nothing" (6:63).

Although we are careful not to interpret Adam's lack of action as sin, we must acknowledge that neither was he walking in obedience to the command of God to partake. His lack of response was a hindrance to the growing and maturing God desired for him. His intention would leave him vulnerable to the voice of the enemy, weak in resisting the desires of his own flesh and eventually would lead him to overt sin and rebellion against the known will of God.

It is important to see that "self" was alive and active before the Fall. Although it was not sinful self, it still needed to be denied. As long as Adam let it rule him, he was powerless to do God's will and fulfill His purpose.

Watchman Nee describes the snare of self for us. Although he speaks after the fact of the Fall, it will help us to understand the danger Adam was in, and how precarious his self-dependence was:

We would like to see how the man first sinned, and receive it as a warning for us today. For as the first sin was, so shall all the sins afterwards be. The sin which Adam committed is the same we all commit. So by knowing the first sin, we may understand all the sins of the world. For according to the view of the Bible sin has but one principle behind it.

In every sin we can see "self" at work. Although people today classify sins into an untold number of categories, yet inductively speaking there is but one basic sin: all the thoughts and deeds which are sins are related to "self." In other words, though the number of sins in the world is indeed astronomical, the principle behind every sin is simply one—whatever is for self. All sins are committed for the sake of self. If the element of self is missing, there will be no sin....It is impossible to mention every sin, but if we were to examine all of them, we would discover that the principle within each one is always the same: it is something that is in some way related to self. Wherever sin is, there is the activity of the self[8]....Self is God's greatest enemy.[9]

"Self," declares Nee, "is God's greatest enemy."

What is self specifically? It takes many forms, some appearing more evil than others. Passivity toward God, a slackness or slowness in responding toward Him, a lack of dependence upon Him, a desire to go our own way and handle our own lives, move in our own wisdom and strength, speak out of our own thoughts, all constitute the self life. A devotion to our own agenda can sometimes look "very good," even "spiritual."

We hear much about "the enemy of our souls," generally referring to Satan. The reality is that Satan can only hook us through our self-center. As such, self is the most dangerous enemy we have. Only dependence upon God's life in us can protect us against self and thus shut the door to Satan as well.

Alone Is Not Good

This, then, was Adam's position. He was commanded to eat of God's provision, but he was not doing so (we are told in Genesis 3:22 that

Adam never did partake of the tree of life), thus his condition was precarious. Understanding all this gives us an important clue regarding what God was about when, following His command to Adam, He says in the next verse, "It is not good that the man should be alone; I will make him an help meet [suitable] for him" (2:18, *KJV*).

Up till this point, as God observed His creation, He pronounced it "very good." But now, something is "not good." What exactly was not good and why?

Adam's being *alone* seems to be the key thought in what God is expressing here. To me, the word "alone" speaks of an inner aloneness. Literally it means "separation."[10] George Berry's *The Interlinear Literal Translation of the Hebrew Old Testament* translates Genesis 2:18 this way: "Not good is being the man to his separation."[11]

The question now becomes, separated from what or whom?[12] At this point, the only other beings present with him were the animals. Earlier we quoted Watchman Nee explaining that Adam had not yet been joined to God in His "divine life." It appears that this statement by God was not a mere observation of Adam's "loneliness," as some have assumed. Rather, far more seriously, it was addressing Adam's relationship with God Himself.

When God said Adam's condition was not good, He really meant it was NOT GOOD! There was a problem in paradise and God, in His infinite wisdom, was going to resolve it. God would bring help. What, or who, would this help be? What kind of help could affect the man's leaning toward isolation and independence? Surely it would take a unique design.

Something to Think About

- What were the two main trees in the garden, and what was the significance of each?
- In regard to the trees, what was Adam commanded to do first? Why was the first part of that command so important?
- Without the tree of life as Adam's source of life, what would be left for Adam?

- 4 -

She Shall Be Called Woman

—*⊙*—

*Then the rib which the Lord God had taken
from man He made into a woman, and He
brought her to the man.*

GENESIS 2:22

A Chinese proverb says, "Women hold up half of the sky."
Ecclesiastes 4:9 states, "Two are better than one."
Proverbs 18:22 tells us, "He who finds a wife finds a good thing."
What was it God intended to bring forth from two that He wasn't realizing with one? What is it that is "good" about a man finding a wife?

In paradise, the Father has declared that Adam's aloneness is not good. He has observed a need and His response is to make a help "suitable" for him. So we read in Genesis 2:21,22:

> And the Lord God caused a deep sleep to fall on Adam, and
> he slept; and He took one of his ribs, and closed up the flesh
> in its place. Then the rib which the Lord God had taken from
> man He made into a woman, and He brought her to the man.

We are told here that God took one of Adam's ribs to make the woman. It is interesting to note, however, that this reference in Genesis is the only time the Hebrew word *sela* is translated as "rib." This particular word is used many times in Scripture as "side" or "side chamber" and is generally an architectural term, referring to the side of an object. In 1 Kings 6:34, this word refers to "two leaves of a door" *(KJV)*.

Conceivably then, according to the *Theological Wordbook of the Old Testament*, this means that when God created the woman by taking a rib, "He took a good portion of Adam's side."[1]

This event was a foreshadowing of another Bride that was to come. The Church, the Bride of Christ, was taken out of the side of Jesus. When the Roman soldiers pierced the side of Jesus with a spear as He hung on the cross, blood and water poured out (see John 19:34). This signified two great benefits of which all believers partake through Christ—the blood for atonement, and the water for purification. Both flowed from our Redeemer's side as He laid down His life to purchase us for His Bride. We came out of His side, He gave us life. We are His body, an extension of His life on earth. As such, we are His own self. The apostle Paul speaks of this when he states, "For we are members of His body, of His flesh and of His bones" (Eph. 5:30).

His Other Self

Even so, the woman was taken from the side of man. She was his own body, an extension of himself. She was, in fact, his other self. Something of Adam's own self was removed from him and returned to him in a very different package.

The woman was not formed of new elements; she was not taken from the dust, hence separate or independent from the man in that sense. She was part of him, his bride, his other self, taken out of him and presented back to him by God, Himself. Adam's first words of exclamation expressed his understanding of this fact as well as his delight:

> "This is now bone of my bones and flesh of my flesh; she shall be called Woman, [*ishshah*] because she was taken out of Man [*ish*]" (Gen. 2:23).

Adam obviously recognized something of himself in her. She was bone of his bones and flesh of his flesh. He welcomed and received her, claiming her as part of himself. This verse is the explanation of the Creation process already told to us in Genesis 1:27. Note the two-step process:

> So God created man in His own image; in the image of
> God He created him; male and female He created them.

First, Adam was created: "God created man in His own image; in the image of God He created him." Second, when the woman was differentiated out of him, "male and female He created *them*" (italics added). When God created Adam, he was created fully in the image of God. When the woman was taken out of him, the image of God was not added to or subtracted from. It was divided. Man was no longer in his original form. Now the image of God was male and female. Yet they were one: "[God] created them male and female...and named them Man in the day when they were created" (5:2, *NASB*).

Because sin (which can be summarized simply as self-centeredness) had not yet made its conclusive entrance, there was no fear or hesitation within them. No one felt threatened. There were no "control" issues, no calculating, no "game playing." They were open, naked and transparent before one another. There was an awareness that God had made them for each other, that He had specifically fashioned this union and there would be an interdependency between them. Although they were two separate beings having very different qualities, their destiny was to be together.

Neil Anderson and Charles Mylander, in *The Christ-Centered Marriage*, express it this way:

> The man is honored by the acknowledgment that the
> woman was created for him. The woman is honored by the
> acknowledgment that the man is incomplete without her.
> In humility, the woman acknowledges that she was made
> for man. In humility, the man acknowledges that he is
> incomplete without the woman. Both share an equal dig-
> nity, honor and worth because of their created purpose.[2]

Leave and Cleave

Now that the woman has been taken out of the man, God further instructs him: "Therefore [because she was taken out of him] shall a

man leave his father and his mother, and shall cleave unto his wife"
(Gen. 2:24, *KJV*).

This directive from God is recorded four times in Scripture. It was
first voiced here, in Genesis 2, repeated by Jesus as recorded in
Matthew 19 and Mark 10, and repeated again by Paul in Ephesians 5.
When a word is mentioned once in the Bible, we need to take special
note. When it is mentioned four times, it becomes a red-flag alert!
God is wanting us to pay very close attention.

—∞—

*The foundation was male and female, the two who
were incomplete without each other, the two who
would together express the image of God.*

—∞—

This union was the beginning point of God's family, the emerging of
the foundation of the House of the Lord and what would ultimately
become the Church. We are seeing unfold before our eyes a micro-
cosm of the structure God chose to use on earth to display His glory
and make His presence known. The foundation was male and female,
the two who were incomplete without each other—the two who
would together express the image of God. Out of this inaugural union,
His glorious purposes will unfold and be manifest. Indeed, this is a
mystery, just as Paul said:

> Husbands, love your wives, just as Christ also loved the
> church and gave Himself for her, that He might sanctify and
> cleanse her with the washing of water by the word, that He
> might present her to Himself a glorious church, not having
> spot or wrinkle or any such thing, but that she should be
> holy and without blemish. So husbands ought to love their
> own wives as their own bodies; he who loves his wife loves
> himself. For no one ever hated his own flesh, but nourish-

es and cherishes it, just as the Lord does the church. For we
are members of His body, of His flesh and of His bones.
For this reason a man shall leave his father and mother and
be joined to his wife, and the two shall become one flesh.
*This is a great mystery, but I speak concerning Christ and
the church* (Eph. 5:25-32, italics added).

The union between the man and woman was to be inseparable; it
was not to be divided. They were to truly know intimacy in the fullest
sense of the word, far beyond what we often think of as the "one flesh
relationship," the sexual union. Sexual intimacy was given to be the
seal, the celebration, of a much greater (and much more difficult to
achieve) intimacy, which was intended to follow—that of heart, soul
and spirit. This kind of relationship would reflect, not only union with
one another, but also with God. It is a mystery, yet God designed that
something of Christ's love—His commitment and faithfulness to us,
His bride, and our union with Him—would be displayed in the marriage union. It would showcase to the world His care and provision for
His own and the high place of honor He has prepared for us.

As Christ cleaves to the Church, nourishing and cherishing her, in
the same manner the man is to cleave to his wife. There is, however, a
further purpose in the man's cleaving, as we shall see.

The Hebrew word for cleave is *dabaq,* which means "to cling, stick
to, follow closely, or join to."[3] Often in the Old Testament, it is used of
physical things sticking to each other, such as the tongue sticking to
the roof of a parched mouth. It also carries the sense of clinging to
someone in affection and loyalty. The Israelites were told to cleave to
the Lord their God in affection and loyalty if they were to receive His
blessing (see Deut. 11:22).

Webster defines the meaning of "cleave" as "adhering to, to be
faithful." This speaks to me of the word "commitment," which often
causes great fear in the hearts of many today, considering all its con-
notations of faithfulness, steadfastness, reliability and accountability.
All these words are applicable to God's instruction to Adam.

The woman is to become the priority relationship in her husband's
life because of the significance and purpose of this union. He is to
cleave to her, not only for her sake, to nourish and cherish her, but for

his own sake as well. He is not the same as he was; part of himself has been removed. In his cleaving, he receives back to himself that which was taken out.

This truth is boldly stated in Marvin Vincent's *Word Studies in the New Testament* in reference to the Ephesians 5 portion of Scripture previously quoted. As Paul describes the way husbands are to love their wives, Vincent's *Word Studies* translates his words this way: "So husbands ought to love their own wives *since they are their own bodies. He who loves his wife loves himself....*Nevertheless let each one of you in particular so love his wife *as being his very self*" (vv. 28,33, italics added).[4]

Clearly, these verses are referring to the first man, and removing the woman out of him. The husband is to cleave to his wife, acknowledging that, in marriage, what was taken out of him long ago in Adam is being returned to him again—to help him.[5]

Help in Time of Trouble

What would be the significance of this help? Are we making too much of the fact that the woman was given to help the man? I think our questions are answered by the meaning of the word "help" itself.

—⁓—

Some have assumed...that the woman was merely brought forth to enable procreation, thereby resolving Adam's solitary condition. Nothing, however, in the Hebrew definition of the word for "help" would remotely refer to the act of reproduction.

—⁓—

"Help," or *ezer* in the Hebrew, means "to surround, to protect, to aid, succor."[6] Webster's definition of succor is "help, to run under, to give aid or assistance in time of distress." "Help" or *ezer* is an extremely strong word, used 21 times in Scripture. Sixteen times it refers to divine help (God Himself), five times to human help, but always in the context of help in time of trouble, help from one's enemies. The word itself tells us of the seriousness of Adam's situation and the critical importance of the resolution God would bring.

The *Theological Wordbook of the Old Testament* says, "While this word designates 'assistance' it is more frequently used to designate 'the assistant' (as with Eve). As to the source of help, this word generally is used to designate 'divine help or aid.'"[7] Psalm 121 reflects this definition: "I will lift up my eyes to the hills—From whence comes my help? My help comes from the Lord, Who made heaven and earth" (vv. 1,2). Eve was both human help and divine help because she came from the hand of God.

face to face

We have determined that the help God was bringing the man was to protect him against his aloneness. Some have assumed, then, that the woman was merely brought forth to enable procreation, thereby resolving Adam's solitary condition. Nothing, however, in the Hebrew definition of the word for "help" would remotely refer to the act of reproduction. Others would go as far as to acknowledge that she was to help him with the task of taking dominion over the earth.

Although both of these assumptions contain some truth, they are peripheral and do not begin to touch the primary purpose for which the woman was designed. God was giving the man help for himself, for his own person. God makes it plain when He says, "I will make him an help meet [or suitable] for him" (Gen. 2:18, *KJV*).

"Well, then," some have said, "the woman was created for the man's use, for his pleasure, for his comfort." This seems to be the common interpretation down through the centuries. God, however, is always wanting to move us from a human-centered or self-centered viewpoint to seeing from His perspective—how all things are properly related to Him and His purposes for them. The woman was created for the man's sake, to help him "as to the Lord" (Eph. 5:22).

To gain an accurate understanding of the kind of help she would be and specifically how she was designed to bring assistance to the problem, we again need to look at the word meanings. God did not leave us to engage in guessing games about His purpose for us. He states it clearly in the words He uses.

Often we misquote Genesis 2:18, referring to the woman as a "help-meet" and sometimes even a "helpmate." However, the word translat-ed "meet" by the *King James Version* of the Bible is actually a prepo-sition in the Hebrew. We need to look at this word more carefully.

The word "for" in Hebrew is *neged*, which comes from the root word *nagad.* Dr. Karl Coke, a Hebrew scholar, wrote in a personal let-ter that *nagad* belongs to a cognate word group that conveys the mean-ing "to the front, to the face, or actually 'face to face.'" It means to "stand boldly out opposite." He declares that this word literally means that the woman is to stand "toe to toe, knee to knee, waist to waist, chest to chest, nose to nose, and eyeball to eyeball" with her husband.

In the verb *nagad*'s causative form (meaning someone or something is causing the action—in this case God), the word "for" means to "manifest" (to make clear or evident, reveal or expose).[8] It is translat-ed "declare" 63 times in Scripture and "tell" 222 times (in the *KJV*), obviously denoting verbal communication. It is interesting to note that the name ultimately given to the woman—"Eve"—is taken from a Hebrew word that also denotes verbal communication. Her name *Chavvah* means "life-giver," but the verb form is "chavah," which is consistently translated as "declare" or "shew" verbally.[9]

"*New*" *Discoveries*

Scientists in our day are just discovering what God tells us about women before He made the first one: Women, in general, would be different from men in their ability to communicate, most especially as it relates to their inner person.

Dr. Donald Joy, Professor of Human Development and Family Studies at Asbury Theological Seminary in Wilmore, Kentucky, states that this difference is clearly evident in the brain construction of male and female. In his book *Bonding, Relationships in the Image of God*, he explains that in the sixteenth week of development the brain of male babies is saturated with androgens (male hormones). This hor-monal bath permanently alters the left hemisphere of the brain where the speech production is generally located, as well as the corpus cal-losum, which carries the messages between the right and left hemi-spheres, giving male children "a slight setback." Dr. Joy states, "This modification seems to account for the rather large number of boys, as compared to girls, who become candidates for the speech pathologist's attention when they arrive at school. In some communities these boys outnumber girls by as much as nine to one."[10]

Although speech is located in the left hemisphere, the emotions, he explains, are housed and accessed in the right hemisphere. The alteration to the corpus callosum in males reduces the brain's ability to move quickly and easily between the two sides, one of the results being that it is more difficult for males than females to put words to their feelings. "Males can't talk to themselves across the hemispheres the way [females] can."

Dr. Joy further states, "The findings about this differentiation of the brain are so new we may consider that we are standing on the threshold of an entirely new set of insights about male and females differences. But the early reports seem to underscore our insights here pointing to the absolute interdependence of male and female and their complementarity."[11]

Right about now we can just hear God saying, "If only you would have read the directions." He has always been clear about His intentions for us. We just haven't looked closely enough. Science, man's best effort, is just now catching up and confirming God's truth. At the beginning of time, God spoke the words concerning the creation of woman that would unfold her purpose, words that would tell us how she would be designed, how she would function and what would be important to her.

Let us note that God gave a woman to be the initial help to the man. Not a mother to be over him, to baby-sit him. Not a child to be under him, to be dominated by him. Not even another man who would be so much like him that he would never be challenged beyond his own nature and instincts. She would be a wife—someone who would be like him, yet different. Someone on an equal par—his other self taken from his side—who would stand "boldly out opposite" him and call him forth in a way no one else could. Someone with whom it would be possible to bond more deeply than with any other person.

She was uniquely and specifically designed to stand before him in an intimate, face-to-face relationship. She was designed to talk to him, to comfort, encourage, confront and challenge him in love, using life-giving words. God intended her to surround and protect something of

His creation that was very precious in His sight: the heart of man—his thoughts, his feelings, his inner self.[12]

King Lemuel's mother understood the purpose of woman and counseled her son:

> An excellent [virtuous] wife, who can find? For her worth
> is far above jewels. The heart of her husband trusts in her,
> And he will have no lack of gain. She does him good and
> not evil all the days of her life (Prov. 31:10-12, *NASB*).

These verses tell us that the man who is so fortunate as to have a wife who knows her purpose, a virtuous woman who lives according to God's design for her, "will have no lack of gain"! Or as the *NIV* says, he will lack "nothing of value." What a staggering promise! This verse alone should drive us into God's Word to find out what He means to accomplish in the marriage relationship.[13] (We will discuss this in greater detail in chapter 7, "Hidden Man of the Heart.")

"She does him good and not evil all the days of her life." God had grand plans for the woman He brought forth. He was bringing resolve to what was "not good."

Yet as we have looked back to Genesis and we have discovered the danger the man was in from the beginning of time, we have to admit that things have not improved. The woman was to have helped him, but it did not happen. Not only did she not help him, but she also exacerbated the problem! What went wrong? Why did the plan fail, at least for a time? That will be the subject of our next chapter.

—✺—

Something to Think About

- Explain the larger meaning of the word "rib."
- When Adam recognized Eve as "bone of his bones, and flesh of his flesh," who was he saying she was?
- What do the words "help" and "for" tell us about the way a woman was designed to function with her husband?

- 5 -

The Strike

—⌇—

Now the serpent was more cunning than any beast

of the field which the Lord God had made.

GENESIS 3:1

This nation will never forget the day in 1986 as we watched, first with excited anticipation and then with stark horror when, 74 seconds after liftoff, the Challenger spacecraft suddenly burst into flames and smoke. Carrying precious lives, it exploded with a force of such intensity that debris rained into the ocean below for an hour.

Standing in the crowd of those watching at Cape Canaveral were parents, husbands, wives and children of those on board. The stunned disbelief and grief that registered on their faces expressed the hearts of Americans everywhere. What had gone wrong? How could something so powerful, so carefully designed, go so horribly awry?

Thousands of years before the Challenger disaster, God's carefully designed plan for humanity similarly went awry right after it started. We know that God was not caught off guard at the terrible turn of events that took place in the garden. Yet down through the centuries, generations of His followers have looked back to the first three chapters of Genesis with the resulting wreckage of lives and wondered, *why?*

Remember the provision of God for Adam and Eve. He had placed them in a perfect environment, given them a mandate of purpose and supplied everything they would need to accomplish it. How could a plan so beautifully put together, so powerful in its design, go so far off course?

> Now the serpent was more cunning [subtle and crafty] than any beast of the field which the Lord God had made. And he said to the woman, "Has God indeed said, 'You shall not eat of every tree of the garden'?" (Gen. 3:1).

Satan, who we learned had led a rebellion against God in the heavenlies and was thus cast from his high estate (see Ezek. 28:16), now continues his rebellion on earth. He makes his appearance in the form of a serpent and introduces to Eve the mere suggestion that perhaps God is withholding something from her.

Eve immediately responds:

> "We may eat the fruit of the trees of the garden; but of the fruit of the tree which is in the midst of the garden [the tree of knowledge of good and evil], God has said, 'You shall not eat it, nor shall you touch it, lest you die'" (vv. 2,3).

Continuing his cunning dialogue Satan declares:

> "You will not surely die. For God knows that in the day you eat of it your eyes will be opened, and you will be like God, knowing good and evil" (vv. 4,5).

Eve begins to reconsider his suggestion, taking closer notice of the tree. *Perhaps God is withholding something; perhaps He really isn't trustworthy. Perhaps there is a better way, a quicker way, something more that I need to help me fulfill my purpose. Just look at the tree— it looks good for food, it's pleasant to the eyes, and a tree desirable to make one wise.* So moving in her own wisdom, outside the expressed word and will of God, "she took of its fruit and ate. She also gave to her husband [who was] with her, and he ate" (v. 6).

It was a coup, a masterstroke, a bull's-eye! Satan had accomplished his purpose. He had conclusively separated them from the one source of life that was stronger than he. He turned them to their own wisdom, their own way, the way of the flesh, in which "nothing good dwells" (Rom. 7:18). He had turned them *to themselves as the centers of their lives.*

Both Adam and Eve needed the tree of life to fulfill their destiny. Both, however, chose their own way. They would be powerless, now, to handle Satan, or to fulfill the mandate God had given them for their own lives.

"You Gotta Serve Somebody"

This act of turning from God's rule to what they perceived as their own, established the world system over which Satan, as god of this age, would actually preside, that being his goal all along (see 2 Cor. 4:4; 1 John 5:19). At this point, like the Challenger spacecraft, life as God had purposed it began to disintegrate, ultimately plunging all of creation into the dark sea of humanity's self-centeredness (see Rom. 8:20,21).

—⁂—

God intended for Adam and Eve, like Jesus, to choose His Spirit (tree of life) as their source of life and wisdom, rather than their own experience of good and evil.

—⁂—

Fear, separation, mistrust, blame and myriad other emotions and attitudes were now a part of Adam and Eve's world. They scurried to cover themselves, to hide from the presence of God. Can you imagine the disbelief and horror that was now registering in the hearts and minds of these two as their eyes were opened to know good and evil? Having partaken of it, eaten of it, having chosen it as their source of life, they now had an intimate knowledge of it deep within their being. Life would never be the same.

It is important to note that God never intended they should not know the *difference* between good and evil. Isaiah 7:15 tells us that when Jesus—the pattern Man—came, He would know how to "refuse the evil and choose the good" at an early age. God intended for Adam and Eve, like Jesus, to choose His Spirit (tree of life) as their source of life and wisdom, rather than their own experience of good and evil.

Now, living from their self-centers, what they judged to be good or evil would be determined by the immediate effect it would have on them. Whatever felt good, or comfortable, or would ensure preeminence, would be good. Pain, discomfort, challenge, anything that would diminish self, would be considered evil. All of life would now be ordered from this perspective.

Although Bob Dylan is no prophet, the title of his song "You Gotta Serve Somebody" is a divine truth. By choosing their own way, Adam and Eve actually came under Satan's rule. They changed kings and kingdoms. The kingdom of darkness was now their abode, and every descendant after them would be born into it (see Rom. 5:12).

The Design Disintegrates

It would be good for us to look a bit at the results of Satan's coup. Because we have already discovered what life was supposed to be like for the man and woman, it shouldn't surprise us that, at this point, it took a 180-degree turn. The fruit of their action was instantaneous: broken relationship. Satan had struck at the core, the very heart of the plan of God. We see the devastating results displayed the world over, down through the centuries, especially as it relates to women.

Woman, we learned, was the man's other self, who he was to nourish, cherish and to whom he was to cleave. She was given from the hand of God to help him, to be to his front, face to face with him, equal to him, to speak to him life-giving words.

Given this information, it assaults our sensibilities, then, to see women denigrated since the earliest times. Instead of being understood to be a help to the man, she has been seen, at best, as rather an infringement on his freedom, albeit one that should be tolerated and even graciously indulged in her little idiosyncrasies (like needing to talk) because "that's how women are."

In worst-case circumstances, woman has been seen as a servant to the man's flesh, used and abused to satisfy his carnal appetites. Even today, women in India are being burned to death in "bride-burnings" because of inadequate dowries. In other countries, young girls are being sold as chattel to wealthy men, only to be discarded as mere refuse when their husbands tire of them.

Sexual mutilation, the "circumcision" of women's genitals, which consists in some cases of large parts of their genitalia being cut away so that intercourse will be extremely painful for them, is still a common practice in some cultures. The purpose is to guarantee that they will remain virgins until marriage. The fact that sex will be excruciating for them the rest of their lives is of no consequence.

It is easy in the United States to forget how women are treated in some countries of the world. We would do well to remind ourselves that women, as yet, have not been received and returned to the position for which God has created them. Incredibly, in the United States, settled by Christians, women were not considered smart enough to have equal voting rights until 1920. A well-known household encyclopedia tells us, "In colonial and early-19th century America, as elsewhere in the world, women commonly were regarded as inferior beings. Their children, property, and earnings belonged by law solely to their husbands....In most respects American women were legally on a par with criminals, insane persons and plantation slaves."[1]

Lest we think the Church itself would not be party to such attitudes, note the commentary of a highly regarded theologian who is widely quoted to this day. Concerning women he says,

> [The woman] was made subject to [the man] because she was made for him, for his use, help and comfort. And she who was intended to be always in subjection to the man should do nothing, in Christian assemblies, that looks like the affectation (pretense) of equality....[She is to be] under the power of her husband, subjected to him, and inferior to the other sex.[2]

We acknowledge that in relatively recent times great strides have been made to give the woman dignity and honor in the Church, but we do not yet fully understand her unique purpose as designed by God. As a result, the Body of Christ is still suffering loss, and Satan is yet robbing the Church of something critical to its welfare.

Satan's Objective

When Satan moved to derail the man and woman, he struck directly at the center of their identity—their maleness and femaleness. It's noteworthy that before Adam and Eve hid themselves from God in the garden they covered themselves from each other; they covered the parts of themselves that identified them as male and female. They became driven by their self-centers. Who they were and how they were designed to function would now become confused, twisted, deceptive, hidden and self-serving.

—⟁—

Satan ultimately purposed to silence the woman, to render her useless and powerless in the man's life. This would rob man of the help God had so carefully designed for him from the beginning of time.

—⟁—

We have seen men—instead of serving their wives and receiving them in the intended place in their lives—seek to use them, objectify them or patronize them. Thereby they are keeping their wives at a distance so that the safety of their own inner isolation is never challenged or threatened. It's not difficult to understand how these attitudes of inequality and disrespect have nullified the effectiveness of the intended role God has given to women in the lives of men, and to recognize what Satan's objective has been in all of this.

It was not just happenstance that the enemy approached the woman first in the garden. He had been present when God spoke His words of intent for the man and woman. He knew she had been called to be a help for the man. Satan's goal has always been to exalt himself above God, to disrupt the plan of God any way he could. It seems obvious that by approaching the woman first, his intent was to attack the help God had sent. Thereby Satan hoped to undermine or weaken the whole of

God's plan. Satan ultimately purposed to silence the woman, to render her useless and powerless in the man's life. This would rob man of the help God had so carefully designed for him from the beginning of time.

The Desire of the Woman

How has woman been affected by the Fall? Has her choice to live by her own knowledge of good and evil affected her as dramatically as it did man? God gives us the answer immediately following her action:

> To the woman He said: "I will greatly multiply your sorrow and your conception; in pain you shall bring forth children; your desire shall be for [to] your husband, and he shall rule over you" (Gen. 3:16).

This is a key verse for all women. I believe God is revealing to us the root of all dysfunctional behavior in women toward men, and where her heart is the most vulnerable to deception. Today we have a new word for it. We call it "codependence." God identified it at the beginning of time and called it the "desire" of the woman.

Scripture tells us that "the woman being deceived, fell into transgression" (1 Tim. 2:14). That is, she did not—with malice and forethought—shake her fist in the face of God and rebel against Him in that sense. She said to God, "The serpent deceived me, and I ate" (Gen. 3:13). This was not "passing the buck," as some have suggested. It was simply the truth. She had believed Satan when he said the tree was good and that she was doing a good thing. The fact that she was deceived is confirmed for us in 1 Timothy 2:14. That same verse tells us that Adam was not deceived. He knew what he was doing and did it anyway. His was an act of treachery. Therefore, the responsibility for sin entering all of mankind fell upon him (see Rom. 5:12).

Eve, however, had her own stumbling block, her own Achilles' heel, which God identifies for us in Genesis. The seeds of Adam's bent toward isolation and independence were there before the Fall, but not fully acted upon (as described in Jas. 1:14,15, sin is always a progression, it is never a sudden act). Thus I believe the seeds of the woman's desire were also there and may have been the attitude that led her to take matters into her own hands. As such, this verse contains a core truth for turning the woman's center.

If you have a *King James Version* or *New King James Version* of the Bible you will notice that the words "*shall be*" in Genesis 3:16 appear in italics. This tells us that they are not to be found in the original text, but have been added by the translators for better continuity or flow of the sentence. In this case, the added words make it sound as though God is commanding Eve: "You must desire your husband, and he must rule over you." Instead, I believe God is stating an observation about her behavior (she is now in her fallen state) and warning her about it. Literally, the verse reads, "Your desire to your husband and he will rule over you."[3]

Some have said that this was part of Eve's penalty for her actions, that her desire for her husband and his ruling over her was God's remedy for her irresponsible, naive behavior. (Much teaching concerning submission uses this verse as its foundation—teaching from the point of the Fall rather than the point of God's original intention at Creation.)

Others have said that this desire was sexual and interpret the passage as though it were some cruel trick of God, in essence saying, "even though childbirth will be painful, yet you will still desire your husband and he will rule you in this area." Still others have said that the woman would innately desire to usurp her husband's authority, that she would strive to take over, to be the leader; but her husband must squelch this tendency and instead he must rule over her.

None of these interpretations touch on what I believe is the truth of this verse. The Hebrew word here is *teshuqah*, which means "desire, stretching out after, a longing."[4] The lexicons do not speak with one voice, however, regarding the root word from which *teshuqah* is derived.[5] Katherine Bushnell (1865-1946, physician, missionary, mobilizer of public opinion against forced prostitution of women, and student of biblical languages), in her book *God's Word to Women*, suggests that an important aspect of the word *teshuqah* is the idea of "turning," a meaning attested in almost all of the early translations of the Hebrew Bible.[6]

Bushnell taught that this word should be translated "turning away."[7] However, I believe that whether we translate the word "desire" or "turning (away)" the same point is made: the woman would have inappropriate desire for her husband because of her lack of trust in God. In essence, God was saying to Eve: "The desire of your heart is turning away from Me to your husband and he will rule over you."

God was telling Eve that man would rule her as a consequence of her turning away from God to him. It was her choice. Had Eve's desire remained upon God, He would have ruled her, which is a privilege God wants to retain for Himself for all His children.

Our "God" Reigns

Whatever we set our desire on will rule us. If we set it on riches, we will make all our decisions and choices based on what will make us wealthy. We will be ruled by riches. If we set our desire on power and reputation, we make our decisions and choices accordingly, perhaps even compromising our own sense of honor. If we set our desire on approval of others, we act in a way that will gain their approval. We will be ruled by the people whose approval we want. Now whether or not these things or people set out to rule us, we will be ruled by them just the same. It is a condition of our own hearts.

You have only to look around you to see how women, even Christian women, set their desire on men. They have turned to them to gain their approval, to be found acceptable, worthy, admired and chosen.

Such is the meaning of Genesis 3:16. You have only to look around you to see how women, even Christian women, set their desire on men. They have turned to them to gain their approval, to be found acceptable, worthy, admired and chosen. As a result, they are ruled by them. They take their cues for life from them. Whatever women believe the male race wants, they will try to become. The greater tragedy of female circumcision, as mentioned earlier, is that it is actually the women who insist on the perpetuation of this cruel practice on their female children. Historically, the women themselves crudely performed the surgery. Without circumcision, said one mother concerning her daughters, "no man will want to marry them. He will think he is getting a girl already used."[8]

Women's obsession with thinness, anorexia, bulimia and the fitness craze all have their roots in this desire. (Men, on the other hand, seem far more interested in impressing other men.)

A plethora of books have been written in the last 15 years addressing this subject as the world itself has suddenly taken notice of this puzzling phenomenon. Books such as *Women Who Love Too Much, The Cinderella Complex, Men Who Hate Women and The Women Who Love Them*, among myriad others, all seek to answer the question: Why does woman look to man for her worth and acceptability to the extent that she will even make self-destructive choices to keep a particular man in her life?

None of these books, of course, look to Genesis 3:16 for their answer. There they would find that this has been the condition of women's hearts, often to their own hurt and ultimately to the detriment of men, since the dawn of time. As a result, they offer other self-centered solutions, such as putting men in their proper place—number two instead of number one—and they write other books such as *Men Are Just Dessert!*

Two can play this game, women reason. *We will objectify men the way women have been objectified and at least the score will be even. Or perhaps we'll just learn to live without them.*

None of the solutions cure the problem, however, and, after all their resolutions, many find themselves back in the counselor's office, "stuck" again.

The Beginning of the End

In spite of living in this "age of enlightenment," with few exceptions, a woman still gets married having unspoken expectations that the man she has chosen will meet all her needs for security, purpose, worth and identity. We may laugh at the "prince on the white horse," but it is evident it is a fairy tale deeply embedded in the heart of nearly every woman.

What a colossal disappointment when this self-centered dream is not realized, when the woman's husband is not able to "fill up the grand canyon" inside of her. Ultimately hurt and disillusionment will set in, followed by anger and then bitterness. A great chasm will develop between them. If one of the partners does not begin to understand God's plan and viewpoint for marriage, they will both become locked into a death spiral in their relating pattern. This empty marriage, devoid of intimacy, may not result in a legal divorce, but the emotional divorce may be just as devastating and destructive to the family. It will take divine surgery to rectify it.

—⚋⚋—

Something to Think About

- How did Satan derail God's plan for the man and woman?
- How has the state of women been affected by the breach in relationship between man and woman that was caused by the Fall?
- Explain how the *desire of the woman* is lived out in her relationships.

- 6 -

Right Expectations, Wrong Source

—∞—

For My people have committed two evils:

they have forsaken Me, the fountain of living

waters, and hewn themselves cisterns—

broken cisterns that can hold no water.

JEREMIAH 2:13

How quickly God's design disintegrated! Satan had struck at the heart of God's plan by striking at the core of our maleness and femaleness. The result was broken relationship and a fracture line running down the center of the foundation of the house of the Lord. We see little resemblance to the exquisite design God fashioned from the beginning to display His image, His love and His glory on earth. What God designed became engulfed in the flames of our own self-centeredness. The debris from that explosion continues its fallout to this day.

We are fashioned for intimacy, we long for love and a sense of true caring. Yet, because of the Fall, we live in a world of broken people driven by our own needs and self-centers. We move toward others, based not so much on what they need, but rather on what *we* need, endeavoring somehow to slacken the hidden thirst deep within our souls.

What is the answer to our dilemma then? Are our longings and expectations so unrealistic that they can never be met in this lifetime?

Dr. Reed Davis addresses our question when, in essence, he says, "It is a question of 'source or resource.' God is our source, others in our lives are resources."[1]

Our need for relationship is legitimate; it is there by God's design. To have healthy, functional relationships, however, it is essential that we sort out what God, our "Source," intended to be to us. Then, as resources, what He intended husbands and wives to be to each other. Truly it will take divine surgery to rectify and reestablish us in the Father's ultimate perspective so that we see things from His viewpoint once again. However, as DeVern Fromke declares, "Before positive restoration can proceed, false foundations must be exposed and destroyed."[2]

Exposed Foundations

One of the foundations being exposed today is the "desire of the woman." Because it is the root of the dysfunctional relationship women have with men, it needs to be uncovered. This needs to be done not only for her spiritual and emotional health, but for his sake as well. Until the desire of her heart is seen for what it is, a heart turned manward rather than Godward, she will be unable to move from her own self-seeking center to the role God has designed for her—that of a suitable help to her husband "as to the Lord" (Eph. 5:22).

The needs women so desperately want met—those for identity, worth, purpose, security and a perfect, unfailing love—are "being" needs. God intended these needs to be fulfilled in each person. Yet the truth is that no person can truly fulfill them in us. They can be met only in God Himself. "In Him we live and move and have our being," Paul declared in Acts 17:28. This must become true in our experience as well.

Since the time of the Fall, the desire of the woman causes her to find her being in man. Man, on the other hand, tends to find his being in his work.

Uncovering the Snare

As stated in the previous chapter, Satan's goal was to separate us from the one true source of life. He wanted to turn us to our own wisdom and ensnare us into living life out of our own "cisterns." He wanted us to believe that, not only could we create our own containers, but then we could also fill them with the water that would satisfy our thirst.

—⟶—

Because she [Eve] was turning away from the living God, the one true source of life, she would now be ruled by the false source of life to which she was turning.

—⟶—

All of us live life from what we truly believe. It is not what we think or know intellectually, but what we are convinced of in our hearts that directs and guides our lives—our actions and reactions. Ultimately, our heart-held beliefs will be evidenced by our behavior. Larry Crabb describes it this way:

> The truth is that everything we do represents an effort to reach a goal that somehow, perhaps at an unconscious level, makes good sense to us. Imbedded in our makeup are certain beliefs about how to become worthwhile or how to avoid injury to our self-esteem, how to be happy or how to avoid pain. Because our fallen nature is naturally attracted to life plans that disregard God, each of us reliably develops wrong beliefs about how to find the meaning and love we need. A belief about what I need implies a goal that I should pursue.[3]

Beliefs, then, determine goals and expectations. Let's reiterate what the desire (*teshuqah*) of the woman's heart is. It is a deep inner longing that is "turning away," and is "stretching out after" the man.

Remember, this was not part of the curse. God was uncovering a snare to Eve. Because she was turning away from the living God, the one true source of life, she would now be ruled by the false source of life to which she was turning.

Whatever we think will satisfy our longing will become our God. Satisfaction found in a wrong source or false god is always temporary, subject to failure and disappointment. False gods are addictive because we must come again and again for refilling and what they can give is never enough. We become slaves to what we think will fill the empty wells inside of us. Our highs and lows are controlled by them. We feel driven, always looking for that elusive someone or something we believe will fill the emptiness.

Evidence of Expectations

The desire of the woman is a heart-held belief. It is the belief that her husband can be her source of life, that he can meet her need for unfailing love, worth, security and purpose. Evidence of this belief is her inevitable disappointment and anger because he can never do it well enough. She tends to view his inability as cold, uncaring and insensitive. Perhaps if she strives harder, does better, she will get the response she desires, but again she is disappointed. Eventually she withdraws, becomes preoccupied with his failures; resentment begins to eat away at her ability to show him affection and the chasm between them widens.

Having entered into marriage believing he was her source, she feels he "owes" her. Although those thoughts may never have been articulated, they are evidenced by her behavior. Anger builds. Eventually it turns to bitterness and ultimately to wrath.

Because she is looking to her husband for her life, he will "rule" her emotionally. She is "up" if things are going well. If not, she is hurt and discouraged, depressed and angry. She is ruled by what he says—if he says it, when he says it, how he says it. Ruled by him—her heart, her "center," having been turned from God to man—she is not able to be the help for him God purposed and designed. She is drinking from a broken cistern. She has the right expectation, but the wrong source.

The wisdom of Solomon expressed in Proverbs 14:12 says it well: "There is a way that seems right to a man, but its end is the way of death." Paul, in Romans 3:23, says, "Everyone has sinned [missed the mark]; everyone falls short of the beauty of God's plan" (Phillips). At the root of our "sinning and missing" is always a heart turned away from God, the one true source of life.

Spiritual Adultery

What is adultery? It is turning away from one's spouse to have a relationship with another. It happens because we believe we are not getting what we want or need from our husband (or wife), so we turn to another source.

—ᴡ—

It is God's ultimate intention to move us from the tree of the knowledge of good and evil—that which we seek in our own understanding to give meaning and worth to our lives—to the tree of life, God Himself.

—ᴡ—

James 4:1-4 is speaking about spiritual adultery as it describes for us how strife originates:

> What leads to strife (discord and feuds) and how do conflicts (quarrels and fightings) originate among you? Do they not arise from your sensual desires that are ever warring in your bodily members? You are jealous and covet [what others have] and your desires go unfulfilled; [so] you become murderers. [To hate is to murder as far as your hearts are concerned.] You burn with envy and anger and are not able to obtain [the gratification, the contentment, and the happiness that you seek], so you fight and war. You do not have, because you do not ask. [Or] you do ask [God for them] and yet fail to receive, because you ask with wrong purpose and evil, selfish motives. Your intention is [when you get what you desire] to spend it in sensual pleasures. You [are like] unfaithful wives [having illicit love affairs with the world and breaking your marriage vow to God!] *(Amp.)*

This sounds like a page out of our lives. As women, many of us look to man, not God, to have our needs met. This is the way that leads to death as far as relationship is concerned. When our expectations are not met in the way we want, it leads to discord, strife and quarrels. When we are not able to obtain the gratification and contentment we feel is due us, we turn away, close our hearts, become disillusioned and angry. From God's point of view we have turned from Him, the true source of life, to seek out other "lovers" who we think will satisfy the longing of our souls. God calls this spiritual adultery, even when the sources we have turned to are our own husbands.

Right Expectations, Right Source

God wants to rectify in each of us the disastrous effects of our heritage in Adam and Eve. We are still unwittingly eating the fruit of their wrong choice. It is God's ultimate intention to move us from the tree of the knowledge of good and evil—that which we seek in our own understanding to give meaning and worth to our lives—to the tree of life, God Himself. DeVern Fromke says, "Until we have truly been cut loose from the old tree; which is wild by nature, and grafted into the good tree, we have not learned to live from our new source."[4]

God wants us to find our *being* needs in Him. Only He can satisfy our need for unfailing love, worth, purpose, identity and security. When we find our life in Him we will discover that we can let go of our demands on others. We can then begin to move in genuine relationship with them because they are not the source of our identity and security anymore. Until this occurs, real intimacy cannot begin to take place.

First Timothy 6:17 admonishes us not to fix our hope on the uncertainty of "riches but in the living God, who gives us richly all things to enjoy." To this a wise teacher responded, "You can tell when you have put your hope in things—riches, people, home, cars, etc.—you stop enjoying them. When we put our hope in God, we enjoy Him and other things as well."

Husband, wife, have you stopped enjoying your mate? If so, this may be an important clue about where you have placed your hope.

A Divine Turning

I want to emphasize strongly that none of what I have said here is intended to negate the fact that many legitimate needs must be met in the marriage relationship for it to function properly. Many critical changes may be needed. What so often trips up a woman, though, is that she has not separated her being needs from her relational needs and looks for all of them from the wrong source and for the wrong reasons. What makes her vulnerable to the deception is that what she wants is "good," even necessary.

—⟪⟫—

When the woman stops looking to her husband for the needs he cannot meet, she frees him to meet the ones he can: the need for intimacy and the shared responsibility for the marriage and family.

—⟪⟫—

Notice in Genesis 3:6 that Eve was tempted to move on her own behalf, not by evil, but by good. The tree that tempted her was "good for food,...pleasant to the eyes, and...desirable to make one wise." All these things God would have given her, but she chose to take them for herself—from the wrong source. Although she was moved by what appeared good, her action was motivated from what 1 John 2:16 describes as "the lust of the flesh, the lust of the eyes, and the pride of life," all of which are "of the world." Right things from the wrong source constitute lust.

The desire of the woman springs from this root; it is a form of lust. It is a way of objectifying the man in her own way, wanting him for herself, to find her life in him. It is looking to him for what only God can supply. As long as her desire is set upon him, the needs she so desperately longs for cannot be met. Even if it were possible for the woman to grasp onto the man and somehow mold him into the image she wants him to be, it would not be enough because lust is never satisfied.

When a woman's heart is turned, when she sets her desire back on God, a new freedom will come. The grasping will be gone from her voice and her attitude. She will be able to move into relationship with him based on wholeness rather than inappropriate neediness, hurt and woundedness. She will be able to speak into her husband's life with more effectiveness because her worth and identity no longer depend on his response. Free now, she is able to be the help to him God designed her to be. (We will discuss this in more detail in the next chapter.)

When the woman stops looking to her husband for the needs he cannot meet, she frees him to meet the ones he can: the need for intimacy and the shared responsibility for the marriage and family.

A Door Unlocks

Let me share with you a key I discovered that can begin to unlock the door to the intimacy you so long for in your marriage. How well I remember the difficult period of time in my own marriage when I was struggling with many of the emotions I have just described. I, too, had come into this relationship with the desire of my heart firmly directed toward my husband. Like so many other women, my thwarted goals to have my needs met in an imperfect man had produced disappointment, pain and ultimately anger (not to mention bitterness and wrath).

Thanks to Dick and Marilyn Williamson, a gifted pastor and his wife, who were being used of God to counsel many couples struggling in cycles of pain, we began to see where our hearts and expectations really were—in each other rather than the Lord. We had stripped away many masks and layers of protective behavior. We had become vulnerable, honest and real, first with ourselves and God, and then with each other. Much forgiveness had been extended, yet it seemed a particular old wound continued to surface in me. I was amazed. I thought that once one forgives from the heart, that was it. It should all be taken care of, the struggle should be over. But for me, this was not true.

Then one day the parable of the servant in Matthew 18 came alive to me in a new way. You know the story. A certain king wanted to settle his accounts. A servant owed him a huge debt; so much, in fact, he was unable to pay it. So the king commanded that he be sold along with his wife, children and all that he had. It would cost him everything, but the debt was so big (according to *The Living Bible*, the equivalent of $10,000,000) that still it would not be enough. The debt would always be beyond a mere servant's ability to pay in full. Throwing himself at the feet of the king, he begged for mercy he did not deserve, and the master, moved with compassion, released him and forgave the debt.

Immediately, however, "that servant went out and found one of his fellow servants who owed him a hundred denarii [$2,000]; and he laid hands on him and took him by the throat, saying, 'Pay me what you owe!'" (v. 28). This was a legitimate debt he was trying to collect; it really was owed to him, but the poor servant had no ability to pay.

I was struck by the similarity in my own life. I owed a debt to my King I could never pay: All the "oughts" and "should haves," all the many ways I have fallen short and continue to fall short in my life. My debt to God consisted of my failure to love Him perfectly. It also consisted of the accumulation of all the failures of a lifetime in which I have not loved others with a perfect love.

Scripture tells us that when we sin against others, we sin against God. David, in admitting his sin against Uriah, prayed, "Against You [God], You only, have I sinned, and done this evil in Your sight" (Ps. 51:4).

My cumulative debt, indeed, was too enormous for me to pay. God could take my life and everything I have and it would not even begin to be enough. Yet on the day when I threw myself at my Master's feet, how graciously, generously and compassionately He released me, forgiving me freely!

Incredibly, though, just like the servant in Matthew 18, I easily forgot how wonderfully I had been forgiven my immense debt. Immediately, in subtle and not so subtle ways, I began to demand payment from those "fellow servants" around me, most particularly from my husband.

We tend to see the debts others owe us—especially our mates—as much bigger than our own. Surely we have done more, loved better, tried harder than they have. Even if that were true, God does not compare our debts to someone else's. He compares our debt to Him to the debt others owe us. Their cumulative debt may be as big as ours, but that's not our business; we can't call in their whole debt. We can only demand the little one that is owed to us. How little it is in comparison to the one each of us owes God!

Notice what happened to both servants. The second one ended up in debtor's prison, but the first servant who would not forgive the small debt was delivered to the "torturers" until he paid back all that was due (see Matt. 18:29,34). How vividly that describes the lot of those who walk in unforgiveness. They are tortured, tormented, imprisoned by their own bitter, resentful thoughts of self-justification and "rightful" condemnation of others. Imaginary arguments flood their minds at the most unexpected times—arguments they always win, the quick-witted death wound ultimately inflicted with the sharp sword of their own bitter words.

When the truth of this passage of Scripture dawned on me, I saw why the cycle of hurt and anger continued to surround our relationship. It wasn't that I hadn't forgiven Howard of past hurts, but as I was struck afresh with the concept of our debt to God and each other, I was taken with a new understanding. Our debt is new every day. Romans 13:8 commands us, "Owe no one anything except to love one another." This is an ongoing, daily debt. We begin every morning with a new debt, a debt of love—"agape" perfect love—to others and they to us, one that we are no more able to fully pay than our old debt. Fortunately for us, God's mercy is new every morning as well (see Lam. 3:22,23).

Suddenly I saw that it wasn't the past hurts I was struggling with; it was the new debt, the fresh expectations that rose in my heart toward Howard each new day as surely as the sun rises in the morning. He still owed me! There was still a debt in my eyes. It hung in the air. It hung over his head. He thought he would never be free, and at that point in our lives he was right. I had taken him prisoner, a prisoner of my expectations. Not only was he not free, but neither was I. Like the two servants in the parable, we were both in prison: he in debtor's prison, I in the prison of my own demands and rationalizations.

Something powerful happened in the spiritual realm the day we took hold of one another's hands and, once and for all, released each other from prison—the prison of demands, expectations and debts.

Graham Greene, an English poet, said: "There is always one moment in childhood [or time] when the door opens and lets the future in." This was that kind of a moment, although we did not know it then.

Just a few simple words allowed the door to open to a whole new relationship. We did not hear trumpets blast, but the heavens seemed to open, along with our hearts! From that day on, the recurrence of that old cycle has been gone.

So what is the answer to our dilemma, to this very legitimate longing for love and intimacy? It is the turning of our hearts to our true

Source. God is desiring to turn both of us, the man and the woman, to find ourselves fully in Him.

I believe this is a key factor in what God is doing today in the hearts of women around the world. In this unprecedented move, He is turning the centers of women, teaching them to deny themselves, their own wisdom, their own strength and to find their Source in God. He is teaching them to live by the "tree of life," the life of God in them. He is freeing them from the broken cisterns of their own making and fashioning them anew, restoring the man's help. Once again, in this final hour, God is moving to present to the man that which was taken out of him so long ago so that what was "not good" will be good again—made whole—for His own sake and purpose.

Something to Think About

- What are our *being* needs? Explain the difference between *being needs* and *relational needs*.
- What determines our goals and our expectations?
- Explain how a woman's belief that her husband should be her source in life would affect their relationship.

Hidden Man of the Heart

—∞—

As in water face answereth to face,

so the heart of man to man.

PROVERBS 27:19 *(KJV)*

One of the most painful and consistent complaints I hear from women as I travel the world is their grief about their marriage relationships. Often I hear them say, "My husband is present in the home physically, but not emotionally—not to me or to the children."

Sometimes they are embarrassed by this complaint, perhaps having been chided by their husbands that they are being unrealistic. Husbands may say that relationship is a "woman thing," not something men should have to be bothered with. Subsequently, these women have determined to try to get along without these heartfelt needs being met. Sometimes they just get busy with the kids, or try to find satisfaction in a job, ministry or friendships with other women. No matter how hard they try, though, the pain and longing won't go away. The fact of the matter is, God didn't intend for it to! God designed woman with an inner need to have an intimate relationship with her husband, one that goes deeper than just the sexual relationship, which at first seemed enough by itself.

At precisely this point, many, if not most, marriages break down. Multitudes divorce. Others, many of them Christians who do not believe in divorce, get stuck here. Unless they discover God's plan and purpose for them, they will live for years in quiet desperation and pain.

The Honeymoon Is Over

Let's examine the dynamics of newly married couples. Two become one, and the honeymoon begins. At first, the union seems like something "made in heaven." As several months pass, more in-depth needs and aspects of the relationship begin to surface. Sometimes we say, in a knowing little chuckle, "the honeymoon is over." What are we really implying by such a statement? Very often it is that the initial aspect of the "one-flesh" union has begun to shift and change for the woman.

It isn't that her physical or sexual desire for her husband is gone, but it will change. Often, at this point we begin to see God's unique design of the woman begin to surface. You see, God has made her in such a way that she cannot function very long at merely a surface sexual level. He has built into her a need to connect—emotionally and relationally—to this one with whom she is being sexually intimate, especially as she begins to mature as a woman. Instinctively she knows, perhaps without being able to articulate it clearly, that marriage will take more than this for it to work over the long haul. (Gary Smalley insists that women "have a marriage manual in their hearts.")

The woman begins to feel the truth of her being in her body. Her sexuality moves to deep within her. It will take more now to interest her in this aspect of their lives. If she is not met on this deeper level, if she continues to give her body without connecting emotionally and spiritually, she can begin to feel used, perhaps even abused. She may start to believe she is being desired for only one reason, that who she is doesn't really matter. In some ways, because there seems to be little contact on any other level, she may start to think she is "prostituting" herself in that she is giving her body without being able to share her real self, the inner person of her heart. The woman yearns to "really connect" with her husband. She wants a union that surpasses just the physical.

The man may be confused, even hurt. He wonders if she no longer finds him desirable. He may wonder, *What in the world has gotten into her?* She says things like, "You don't really care about me," or, "I want a relationship with you."

He thinks they have a relationship and all is well. Her comments don't make sense to him. He feels like the task-oriented young man in

—⚏—

Women naturally find it easy to move in the realm of feelings, readily identifying their own feelings and frequently those of others as well.

—⚏—

the counselor's office who said, "I don't know what she wants from me. I'm responsible, I come home every night, I bring home my paycheck. I'm committed to this marriage!" Thinking for a moment, the counselor responded, "But are you committed to *her?*"

In essence, the woman is knocking on the door of her husband's heart, asking, *Will you come out?* Her own heart cry is, *I need to know you on a deeper level, and I need to know that I am known and cared about on a deeper level too. I want to know what you think and feel, because it is in the "feeling" area of your being—your heart—that your real person dwells.*

God often uses this unrest and dissatisfaction with the status quo in the woman's heart to move the couple to their next level of growth. The wisdom of the woman and the receptivity of the man, however, will be crucial here.

Moving On

George Guilder, in his book *Men and Marriage,* writes that woman's sexuality is far more relational than man's. He calls it "long-term" sexuality and declares, "The crucial process of civilization is the subordination of male sexual impulses and biology to the long-term horizons of female sexuality."[1]

God, for His own purposes, has specifically designed women with an inner need to move past the surface in a relationship, to "get to the heart of things." Women naturally find it easy to move in the realm of feelings, readily identifying their own feelings and frequently those of others as well. This very aspect of her nature is the target of many jokes in our culture. Women are often ridiculed as being too emotional and not logical, as though feeling and thinking were mutually exclusive.

The real truth is that feelings result from thoughts, and if divorced from our emotions, we will have trouble identifying our real thoughts as well (at least in the important issues of life). We should not be controlled by feelings or depend on them as an infallible source of truth. Feelings, however, are important clues that will tell us more about *our truth*—what we really think and believe—than anything else. Our minds may lie to us, but our feelings will give us away every time. When we begin to process our emotions, we discover what we really believe deep inside. This was God's purpose for the woman in the man's life—to bring him out from that inner place of aloneness where he hides from himself and others, even from God. Proverbs 27:19 expresses this truth:

> As in water face answereth to face, so the heart of man to
> man [one human being to another] *(KJV)*.

In the dynamics of relating to one another—husband to wife, friend to friend—we are continually confronted with what is in our hearts. If emotionally isolated from others, we can live to ourselves and never be confronted with the "real stuff" of life in a way that changes our hearts, our selfish motives and actions, or addresses real areas of need, neglect or denial within us.

One counselor said, "If we would respond to the Word and corresponding work of the Holy Spirit, there would be no need for counseling. Our hearts would be conformed to the image of God as we continually humbled ourselves under the promptings of the Holy Spirit. Sadly, however, this is not always the case. We avoid and deny things we don't want to admit or deal with. Sometimes we have 'blind spots' that others see, but for reasons unknown to us, we don't."

As the verse from Proverbs indicates, in the mirrored effect of relationship our true hearts are revealed and self is exposed. This is the help God wanted the man to have when He gave him a wife. As we learned in chapter 4, the woman was especially and specifically designed to live "face to face" with her husband.

Fashioned for Intimacy

First Peter 3:1-6 immediately comes to mind here. It is the so-called "submission verse" often used to silence women and once again render them ineffective in the design of God, when in reality it is saying the exact opposite:

> Wives, likewise, be submissive to your own husbands, that even if some do not obey the word, they, without a word, may be won by the conduct of their wives,
>
> when they observe your chaste conduct accompanied by fear [respect, reverence].
>
> Do not let your adornment be merely outward—arranging the hair, wearing gold, or putting on fine apparel—
>
> rather let it be the hidden person of the heart, with the incorruptible beauty of a gentle and quiet spirit, which is very precious in the sight of God.
>
> For in this manner, in former times, the holy women *who trusted in God* also adorned themselves, being submissive to their own husbands,
>
> as Sarah obeyed Abraham, calling him lord, whose daughters you are if you do good and are not afraid with any terror (italics added).

If we take these verses out of their surrounding context, we would have to conclude that the woman is to be a silent witness to her husband and is, in fact, being commanded to do so. What about our history lesson in which we learned that the woman's purpose—"for" the man—and her name "Eve" were both taken from words that denote speaking? We have some contradictions here.

When asked what were the three most important things to know before buying real estate, an agent responded, "Location, location, location!" The same could be said for understanding Scripture. Where it is located—its context—often gives us the best information.

These verses in 1 Peter are sandwiched in the center of a long exhortation about how we all are to respond in difficult circumstances. The woman is not being told that she is not to speak to her husband about sensitive issues. In context, she is being told *how* she is to speak: without a retaliatory, angry word, just as Christ, "who, when He was reviled, did not revile in return" (2:23). He did not return "evil for evil or reviling for reviling, but on the contrary blessing....For 'He who would love life and see good days, let him refrain his tongue from evil, and his lips from speaking deceit'" (3:9,10).

—⁂—

The heart is the deepest, most inner recess of our being, the place of absolute truth where all masks and pretensions are removed. The heart is the place where the real person dwells.

—⁂—

Jesus was not silent in His interaction with His detractors; He was only silent concerning His own self-defense. He trusted Himself to God, stayed on task and continued to speak the truth without getting ensnared into a defensive, revengeful diatribe with them.

First Peter 3:6 seems to suggest to us that the woman's submission, as one who is adorned with "the hidden person of the heart" (v. 4) might be accompanied by extreme difficulty. She is told that she is Sarah's daughter if she does good and is "not afraid with any terror." What could terrorize the woman?

To answer that question we need to understand more clearly the meaning of "the hidden person of the heart." The heart denotes "thoughts, feelings, mind, middle."[2] The heart is the deepest, most inner recess of our being, the place of absolute truth where all masks and pretensions are removed. The heart is the place where the real person dwells.

A woman whose center has been turned, who abides in the Holy Spirit (who Himself lives in the hidden place of our hearts) can begin to trust that what is going on inside her is from the Lord—that God is giving her insight and understanding. The "marriage manual" God has put inside her heart is beginning to take shape. By exhibiting a gentle and quiet[3] spirit, "settled, not disturbed," because she knows where her confidence is, God is wanting her to bring out these insights, to share them with her husband.

This is not a case of setting herself over the man as his "teacher," as forbidden in 1 Timothy 2:12. This is relationship, sharing her inner self with him in the give and take of normal living as God intended it to be. In this process, however, there may be consequences, and 1 Peter 3:6 is admonishing the woman to be prepared with a proper response. She is not to be "afraid with any terror."

Be Prepared for Reactions

"Terror" in the original Greek denotes "to scare or frighten" and is perhaps akin to a word that means "to fly away,"[4] like a bird that hears a loud noise.

As a woman begins to share her heart with her husband—even if she is gentle and kind—he may immediately become defensive and self-protective. Instinctively he may throw up smoke screens of anger and intimidation. These tactics are an attempt to drive her back so as to protect his inner safety. He wants to keep her away from that inner sanctum where he has been able to hide from his feelings and emotions for many years, probably since childhood. If the woman will stay in relationship, though, stay open and not respond by retreating again into her own inner self-protectiveness, life and healing will eventually begin to come forth.

John and Paula Sandford describe this dynamic in their book *The Transformation of the Inner Man*. Based on their extensive counseling experience they state:

> Companions and counselors must search patiently to find the frozen hearts of their friends. But the most common sign of returning to life is that the warmer the love given, the meaner the response. Fear of vulnerability creates hate. Each stony heart has a life of its own. It sings lies

into the mind....This sign of coming to life is pain, like when our leg has fallen asleep, and the first we are aware of it is when we feel a million pricking needles of pain—the reason is that the leg is coming to life again! But our loved one built that hiding place precisely to escape pain. Therefore the attack is automatic, to remove the menace before the walls crumble altogether....Husbands, more frequently than wives, often become meaner and meaner the more their wives express love. Just so, the transformation of hearts of stone is not accomplished by distant, safe prayers and well wishings. Hearts of stone can only be melted by persistent, pain-bearing hearts willing to lay themselves down daily, understanding and forgiving every time the quarry turns to attack, until the ice thorn melts.[5]

If the woman does not know God's plan in all this, that He is wanting to bring wholeness and maturity to each of them through their relationship, through shared open hearts, she will be frightened by his show of strength. She will then retreat into self-protective silence herself or, in self-defense, she will explode in anger also. If she explodes, her divine gifting of words meant to bring forth life and restoration can become deadly weapons. She can use them like knives, laying her husband open with ridicule and disrespect, doing further damage to an already wounded heart, which can take years to repair.

In essence, then, the woman in 1 Peter 3 is being exhorted to live with her husband as one who has learned to trust in God. As a woman whose desire has been turned from man to God, she is to have courage, to be responsible with her words, to learn to speak with respect even when disagreeing with her husband. In anger, she is not to sin (see Eph. 4:26). She is to learn how to speak "the truth in love" (v. 15), to bind mercy and truth around her neck so that she will "find favor and high esteem in the sight of God and man" (Prov. 3:3,4).

This is a woman who has learned at God's hand, "A wholesome [healing] tongue is a tree of life, but perverseness in it breaks the spirit" (15:4). She knows she is an ambassador of Christ in this marriage: "Death and life are in the power of the tongue, and those who love it will eat its fruit" (18:21). She also knows that, having found her, her husband has found "a good thing," and has obtained "favor from the Lord" (v. 22). Yet, like Esther, she is to learn when to speak, and when silence would be the better part of wisdom.

All this is for her husband's sake, to help him, so that "if [he will] not obey the word...[he] may be won by the conduct of [his wife]" (1 Pet. 3:1). She is to demonstrate before him, through the strength and wisdom of God's life in her, what makes life work. Her example *includes*, not excludes, speaking with life-giving words.

—∞—

[A woman's] submission is knowing her purpose from God's viewpoint and then bringing her whole self to the man for his good, knowing that their destiny is together.

—∞—

As women we need to learn who we are, and that we are to speak as Christ's representatives. A woman who does this, who becomes consistent in it, will discover that eventually the heart of her husband will begin to trust in her. He will also begin to learn for himself how to live adorned with "the hidden person of the heart."

Rules or Relationship?

This is true submission "as unto the Lord." It is more about relationship than it is about authority. Although 1 Peter 3:6 tells us that Sarah "obeyed" Abraham, we should not read it without putting it in the context of their whole life together. The truth is that after they had both matured, after their names (natures) had been changed and the "life" (Isaac) God promised them had come forth by the Spirit, Abraham also obeyed Sarah—at God's command (see Gen. 21:12). She helped him see something he could not see by himself. Theirs was a mutual submission. God is after the interdependence of the relationship, not rules and regulations.

It is a mistake to limit the instruction given in the first six verses of our passage in 1 Peter to women who have unbelieving husbands, as so often has been the case. Sarah's relationship with Abraham is our example, and both were believers.

We can see, then, from these verses in 1 Peter 3 that the woman's submission, like her creation, is initially for the man's sake, to help him. Submission is knowing her purpose from God's viewpoint and then bringing her whole self to the man for his good, knowing that their destiny is together. As the woman begins to walk according to her design with the man, no longer frightened by old methods of rebuff, or returning his angry responses in like manner, it is likely that eventually he will come out of hiding. Relationship will begin to happen between them. It may take some time, but if she knows who she is, if she's patient and consistent, if she learns at God's hand to open "her mouth with wisdom" and have on her tongue "the law of kindness" (Prov. 31:26), things most likely will begin to change.

According to Understanding

This passage in 1 Peter goes on to address the man. The husband is now told how he is to live with this one whom God has given him: He is to "dwell with [her] with understanding, giving honor to the wife, as to the weaker vessel, and as being heirs together of the grace of life, that your prayers may not be hindered" (1 Pet. 3:7).

The man is to understand his wife, the nature and design God has given her for his help. He is not to treat her roughly or in an intimidating fashion. Rather, he is to treat her with gentleness and honor because they are "heirs together of the grace of life" (v. 7). He is to come out of his slumber, his passivity, and awaken to her, for in their togetherness, their unity, their interdependence, God's purpose for them will come forth.

He must not disregard her or cast aside her needs, because God will use something in the very midst of those needs to bring him forth into relationship—with her, with Himself and with others. It is true that only God can give the husband "life" in the eternal sense, but the woman can lead him into life so that even eternal things take on a greater significance for him. If her husband will open to her, if he can receive her and cleave to her in this, he will begin to grow to a greater level of maturity than he has known before. As both are willing to come out of their self-protectiveness—the woman daring to come out of that deep place where she lives, the hidden person of the heart, even at the risk of rejection, and the man coming out to meet her— real maturity begins to take place.

Paul Tournier confirms this thought when he says, "For a person to achieve his or her potential there must be at least one other person with whom he or she is totally open and feels totally safe at the same time."[6]

John Powell says, "As we begin to share ourselves with another, invite another to share his or her self with us—as we learn to resolve conflicts as they arise—we will grow up."[7]

The reality is, for us to stay hidden and self-protective is to remain developmentally arrested, living life in a diminished way, often at an emotionally childish level. Men struggle with this, however, much more than women. Certainly this is why God puts the emphasis on the woman being the help for the man in this area and not the other way around. Indeed, He has fashioned her for this very purpose.

Real Men Do

All of life seems to conspire in keeping the man in a hidden and thus emotionally occluded condition. Here again we see the ploy of the enemy. Surely society plays right into Satan's hands as he strikes early to hinder what God had on His heart from the beginning.

Perhaps the most frequent message to male children is, "Be a big boy; big boys don't cry. Be tough!" Childhood wounds, rejections, betrayals and humiliations, some of which are devastating, all must be buried in the heart of a young boy if he is to survive in a "man's world." From the beginning, the message is that "being a man" is not to be a feeling person.

Daphne Rose Kingma, in her book *The Men We Never Knew*, states:

> Men have had to kill the wild beasts, fell the forests, sail the seas, wage the wars and build the skyscrapers in order to secure the progress of civilization. To do this required that they set aside their feelings.
>
> Men have been taught that in order to hold the world

together, to make political, economic or social decisions, they have to ignore their emotions because the intervention of "feelings" could make mincemeat of their choices. Thus they have been encouraged not only to not have feelings, but have also been specifically instructed to shove down whatever feelings would surface.[8]

Many men have learned strategies from childhood to protect themselves from the emotions that would label them unmanly or unmasculine, and now as adults they have perfected them. Workaholism, alcoholism, preoccupation with sex, money, power, position, recreation, TV or just plain passivity are ways men have learned to hide from the real issues of life, and thus from the people who are supposed to be closest to them.

What is the danger of this? Why has God said it is "not good"? Because such self-protectiveness carries an enormous price tag. When we refuse to feel, we alienate from ourselves and, as a result, we alienate from others as well. To have a true relationship with someone we must bring an authentic, feeling self—to God and to others.

The ripple effect of man's isolation has been staggering. The home, family, church and nation are rocking in the wake of man's emotional abandonment, today more than ever before. We desperately need men who will feel, who will get involved, who will face into the pain of life, letting it touch them at the core of their being and yet, by the grace of God, not be overwhelmed by it. Our welfare depends on man's ability to live in relationship and intimacy with his wife, children and others. To do that there needs to be healing, restoration—help—which the Lord has given.

A man whose heart has begun to trust in his wife will gain courage to share with her the wounds and failures of the past. As these wounds and failures are brought out into the open, into the light of relationship, real healing can begin to take place. Those years can be left behind forever as he discovers that he is truly loved. Oh, not for some image he felt obligated to project, but for the person he really is. Fallible and limited? Yes. Needing to grow? Yes. What freedom, though, when he discovers that imperfection is the condition of all of us in this life and we can love and be loved anyway! The voices of the past that were interpreted through a child's perspective can be seen for what they were—someone else's imperfection being targeted at us. Liberated from himself, no longer needing to hide and protect, a man becomes free to reach beyond himself to others, and a new day is born.

Truly, God has put us together in a most precious and purposeful way.

Something to Think About

- Explain the context of 1 Peter 3:1. What is really being said here?
- Describe true submission.
- What is essential to our emotional (and spiritual) maturity?

- 8 -

Unmasking the Accuser

—⚏—

"The accuser of our brethren,...has been cast down."

REVELATION 12:10

The playroom was full of activity. Cade and his little friend Bronti, both four, were excitedly setting up house in a large, newly acquired cardboard appliance box.

Bronti was busy doing all the things wives do. She was organizing furniture, making sure the pint-size table and chairs were just right. She was fixing plastic peas and potatoes for lunch, at the same time making sure all the doll babies were happy and cared for. "Come and eat," she called from the cut-out window.

Cade, however, did not have food on his mind. He had more important "manly" things to do. He had donned his Batman cape and was leaping off the playroom couch, slaying the imaginary enemies that were attempting to invade their home. He was "flying" through the house, coming in the window and going out the door. He was stopping only long enough to apply a few quick karate chops to the top of the playhouse roof. Surely any wife would be impressed with such exploits. Apparently not in this instance, though.

Soon, Cade's mother could hear Bronti's first tentative plea: "Husband?" Then, more emphatically, "Husband!" Still undaunted, Cade showed no signs of slowing down. Finally, her frustration mounting and clearly irritated she exclaimed, "Husband! Husband! You're not doing it right!"

As my friend related this story to me, I couldn't help but think how early the expectations start, and how abundant are the opportunities to hear in each of our hearts, *You're not doing it right!*

Checked Your ID Lately?

Even at the tender age of four, something about an accusation seems to go straight to our hearts. Words—words spoken by parents, teachers, peers and even strangers—begin to form a picture in our hearts of who we are.

Sometimes the messages are not words. Sometimes they are just looks—looks of disapproval, disgust or rejection. Or they are messages of touching—the inappropriate kind, such as slapping, beatings or sexual abuse.

Sometimes the messages are derived from what *is not* there—no words, no looks, no touching. Sometimes it is just the gaping absence of nurture and care by one or both of the key caregivers in our lives, through physical or emotional abandonment. The automatic interpretation of this message by default is that we are unworthy of another's love and attention.

Then there is the message of our culture, the standards of acceptability communicated loudly and incessantly, day after day, through the media: television, magazines and newspapers. "This is how you must look—slim and sharp!" "This is what you must have—the latest clothes, the new car, the tasteful home!"

Psychologists say that by the time we reach our teenage years each of us has, for the most part, formed our core beliefs about ourselves. By then, based on our interpretation of the messages around us, we have decided whether we "measure up," and our identity as a person is generally firmly in place. This is now "who we are," and for many that evaluation will never be questioned again. Any new information will be processed through that belief system, and will simply cement what we already "know."

It is normal to form our pictures of ourselves from the messages we receive around us. God intended it to be that way—that who we are would be mirrored by others in our lives, affirmed and confirmed by them. God intended that we would communicate to each other God's truth about us, "the edifying of itself [each other] in love," as Paul states concerning the growth of the body in Ephesians 4:16.

In the perfect, unfallen world God planned, all the voices in our lives would have been positive, but we don't live in such a world today. Our world is broken, full of broken people, who take out their brokenness on others. Added to that, we interpret life through our own broken psyches.

—∞—

The inner picture we have formed of ourselves has been gravely distorted. Yet all our behavior patterns, our ways of relating to others, even our way of relating to God will be based on this picture formed early in our lives.

—∞—

Those who have had thoughtful, loving parents are indeed fortunate. For those so blessed, perhaps the damage won't be as deep. Parents, however, are not the only voices in our lives and sometimes, for some children, the other voices are louder. As a result, for many (if not most) of us, the inner picture we have formed of ourselves has been gravely distorted. Yet all our behavior patterns, our ways of relating to others, even our way of relating to God will be based on this picture formed early in our lives.

The Thief of Intimacy

Enter the master tactician—the "accuser of the brethren"—whose chief job is to rob, kill and destroy through deception what God has created to satisfy His own heart: a family who would relate intimately with Himself and others.

He comes early in our lives, and he comes purposefully. A creature devoid of honor, his intent is to cripple us in our youth when we are the most vulnerable, the most insecure, and thus the most susceptible to his lies. He knows that if he can distort the picture, we will reject ourselves out of hand, go into hiding, and never become the transparent, authentic people God designed us to be.

The *Spirit-Filled Life Bible* defines Satan as, "An opponent, or the Opponent; the hater; the accuser; adversary, enemy; one who resists, obstructs, and hinders whatever is good."[1]

Revelation 12:9 calls him, "that serpent of old, called the Devil and Satan, who deceives the whole world." His other name, "devil," describes his slanderous actions more specifically. The word "devil" (*diabolos*) comes from the verb *diaballo*, which means "to defame, slander, falsely accuse."[2]

Remember, in chapter 5 we said that Satan's goal in turning Adam and Eve from the tree of life to the tree of knowledge of good and evil was to entice them to live by their own life rather than God's life. He knew that if he could turn them to themselves, they would have no power against him, and he would be safe. Only as they focused on God and lived by His life could they accomplish God's purposes and be of any danger to Satan.

Although we are on the other side of redemption, Satan uses the same tactic. If he can't steal our salvation, he knows he can cripple us for God's purposes if he can again cause us to become self-focused.

Genesis 3:1 tells us that the serpent "was more cunning than any beast of the field." When he came to ensnare Eve by pointing out that the fruit from the forbidden tree of knowledge would make her "be like God, knowing good and evil" (v. 5), he was implying that God had not given her everything she needed for this life. She needed something else to fulfill what she lacked.

In essence, the serpent was saying, "To be fulfilled and successful in life, you need to be more than you are. Someone else is higher and greater than you, and this is not acceptable. This means you are deficient. The God who made you cannot be trusted to make you enough. The tree of life—God's life—is insufficient for the task. What you need is something from the world—the tree of knowledge of good and evil—to make you enough."

Satan's message, in effect, was,

- You are not enough.
- God is not enough to make you enough.
- You need something from the world to make you enough.[3]

One of Satan's most effective tactics is to mix truth with his lies. His first implication was true, and something in each of us knows it. In ourselves we are not sufficient. The other two suggestions, though, are pure lies. Satan knew, however, that if he could get Eve stuck on the implication that she needed to be more, that somehow she had been short-changed, he could lure her into taking action on her own behalf.

Satan's intent was to convince Eve that she was the important player in the program and, in her mind, this probably included Adam as well. *Maybe the serpent is right,* she may have thought. *Maybe what God has planned to accomplish depends on us, and on our adequacy, on some goodness or power within ourselves.* Eve believed the lie. She reached out with her own hands to make up the deficit she perceived to be in her. Adam soon followed. We all know the drastic results. By believing the lie, by focusing on themselves, the bridge between them and their true Source of Life was broken.

Now, wholly dependent upon themselves, what had been only a perceived deficiency became a true one. They were naked! They were exposed! They were in danger of being rejected and abandoned forever! The shame was too much. Not only were they now ashamed before God, but they were also ashamed in front of each other. They ran to make coverings with their own hands to hide their nakedness, coverings that could never bring them the sense of innocence and acceptance they had once known. Ultimately they hid among the trees.

This attempt to make up their perceived deficit by their own efforts was the precursor of all sin, all hatred, all murder, all self-seeking, all hiding that is present in the world today.

Two Kinds of Shame

The Bible calls this sense of fear of being found naked, exposed and ultimately abandoned "shame." Revelation 3:17,18 says, "you are wretched, miserable, poor, blind, and naked—I counsel you to buy from Me gold refined in the fire, that you may be rich; and white garments, that you may be clothed, that the shame of your nakedness may not be revealed; and anoint your eyes with eye salve, that you may see."

God, in His grace, allows us to feel the terrible emotion of shame so that we would be alerted to our sinful condition and go to Him for mercy, forgiveness and a covering for our nakedness. The only effectual covering, the only one sufficient to cover every transgression, is the white garment of Christ's righteousness purchased for us by His shed blood on the cross of calvary.

Another kind of shame, however, is one that feels the same as legitimate shame. It, too, makes us feel afraid—afraid that our deficiency will be exposed; that we will be found naked, and therefore ultimately rejected and abandoned. This is "false shame," the precursor of sin. This is the snare Satan set for Eve in the garden. If he could convince her that something was wrong with her when there wasn't—if he could convince her that the way God made her was lacking and defective, that this life was about her and what she could produce—she would become self-focused and look to herself to make up the difference. This, in turn, would lead her away from her true life source, thus causing her to sin and experience a true sense of shame.

Satan uses this same tactic today, and it is the cause of all the havoc in the world. Christians are not exempt. They are probably his most specific target. Satan came to Eve with this lie before the Fall, before there was any sin, and after our sins are forgiven he comes to us telling the same lie.

Soon after the first wonderful blush of our salvation begins to wane—perhaps this process is actually the *cause* of its waning—we begin again to look around us, to see how we "measure up." "See," whispers the enemy, "you still don't have it. Other Christians look better, pray better, talk better, understand Scripture better. They have more victory over their sins. Their children are all well behaved and serving the Lord. The blood of Jesus may get you to heaven, but here...No, you're still not enough."

The self-focus renews with vigor. All the old self-protective instincts that worked in the world kick into gear. We just dress them up better, put them inside "church clothes." Their purpose is still the same. It is to keep people at a distance so they will not discover the painful, terrible "truth" about us—we are still inadequate!

The message of false shame is not connected with sinful things we have done. It is an accusation about who we are at the core of our being: We are flawed, defective, unacceptable, lacking in whatever it takes to make life work. With it is the accompanying belief that others *do* have it together, that they have figured it out, that they have

—∞—

The older we get, the more resources we have to make better coverings. Now, we finely hone the instinctive, self-protective strategies we developed earlier in life to camouflage our perceived lack.

—∞—

what it takes. One can hear the pathos in Keith Miller's words when he describes this struggle in his own life: "It was as if everyone else had received a manual about how to get along and be loved and at home in life," he writes, " and I hadn't got one."[4]

Hide and Seek

So the game becomes: What can I do to keep others from discovering my terrible secret? We do the same thing Adam and Eve did when they believed the lie. We try to make up the deficit with our own wisdom. The more we try, the more we realize how inadequate our own efforts are. We become more fearful, more afraid that our nakedness will be exposed.

The older we get, the more resources we have to make better coverings. Now, we finely hone the instinctive, self-protective strategies we developed earlier in life to camouflage our perceived lack.

We dress better, drive a better car, talk a better game, get nicer (or meaner and more controlling, if that serves our purpose). We join more committees, serve on the right boards, get more degrees, work harder, try to amass more money. Or we drop out all together: we drink, do drugs, eat, get depressed or just vegetate in front of the television. One thing is certain: We never tell anyone what is really going on inside of us.

None of it produces the rest and acceptability for which we are looking. Ultimately, just like the Israelites who were also looking to the world (Egypt) for their provision, we discover that "the bed [of our own making] is too short for a man to stretch himself on and the covering too narrow for him to wrap himself in. [All their sources of confidence will fail them]" (Isa. 28:20, *Amp.*).

This knowledge doesn't cause us to give up, however. Instead, it just makes us work harder to shore up our hidden place.

The Baggage We Bring

Many of us bring this mentality, this distorted, self-focused, defective view of ourselves into relationships—perhaps most significantly that of marriage—along with the accompanying masks. This perception causes "the hidden person of the heart" to *stay* hidden at all costs.

If we are fortunate, God will allow, and perhaps even orchestrate, events in our lives that will ultimately force us into a crisis so severe that all our lifelong, carefully constructed defenses will begin to crumble. Someone said, "When the pain of staying the same becomes greater than the pain of change, we will change."

That is what happened to my husband, Howard, and me.

In my first book, *Inside a Woman*, I described some of the circumstances in my life that had influenced the opinion I had formed of myself. My parents were wonderful people, but they were very busy. My father was a pastor; my mother had all the never-ending duties of a pastor's wife. Their generation was not as aware of how vitally important closeness and communication are to a family, as we have since become.

I interpreted their lack of time and little overt affection for me as a negative statement about my worth and acceptability. (Satan will use whatever he can.) I developed masks of perfectionism in many areas of my life. I tried hard to be the best in all of them—supermom, best wife and perfect homemaker, among other things. I hoped that if I could do what I did well enough, no one would notice the many other flaws I was so sure I had.

Howard was chronically ill as a child because of allergies and sinus problems. He was chubby as a young boy, and although he lost weight later in high school and felt some sense of achievement when he became proficient at tennis, by then the feeling of unacceptance was already in place.

He, too, was raised in a pastor's home. At that time, many pastors were taught that their ministries came first. The needs of the church took priority over the family. They moved a lot—particularly difficult for Howard, who was very shy. Raised during the Great Depression, money was at a premium. Being poor simply added to his low evaluation of himself.

Like me, Howard also developed masks—masks to keep the world from finding out what an unacceptable, terror-stricken person lived inside of that together-looking, seemingly normal body of his.

He could have related well to Don Hudson, coauthor of *The Silence of Adam*, who writes, "For years, I pretended I was adequate. But I was playing a game. There were, in my past, devastating circumstances that told me I was deficient. To admit such a deficiency, however, meant death for me. Even though I felt inadequate in everything, I put up a competent front. I was a little boy in a man's suit."[5]

Howard could have written those words. He appeared to be happy and friendly. He had great verbal skills. He could hold his own on almost any topic (and frequently take the lead). When we met, he appeared to have "the world by the tail." I was instinctively drawn to his air of confidence, especially because I had so little of my own. Perhaps he had enough for both of us.

We would discover later that each of us had married masks, the images we wanted to project to be acceptable. No doubt, underneath, something of ourselves had drawn us together, something we loved, but the masks were strong and firmly in place. So strong, they threatened to destroy our marriage.

Like the men we mentioned in the previous chapter, whenever I, or others, tried to get close to Howard, he would throw up a smoke screen of intimidation and anger to keep us away. As a result, intimacy and relationship were impossible for him.

Proverbs 18:19 vividly describes his plight when it says, "An offended brother is worse than a fortified city. His contentions (quarrels, strife) are like the bars of a castle."[6] One who has been offended (and that includes most of us) has built a strong, fortified hiding place. The person is like a city that has impregnable walls, specifically built to keep intruders out. The person's contentions (arguments, anger, strife) are like the bars of a castle, added tactics that ensure no one will get inside that inner place, the "castle," where he or she lives. Tragically, though, the impenetrable defenses the person has erected, the masks so carefully designed to protect, also imprison him or her.

This describes Howard, and many others like him. In his mind, his life depended on keeping people from getting too close. If they really found out who he was—flawed, defective, unacceptable—surely everyone would leave, and he would live in isolation forever. He did not know he was already living in isolation—deep, inner isolation.

As for me, my need for perfection was extremely threatened by this imperfect marriage. I was more concerned with the "ideal" than the real. I could only think about myself. This marriage—Howard's anger and alternating withdrawal—were a reflection of me and my worth. I did not have the ability to understand the fear Howard was fighting, because I did not understand my own.

It is interesting that in the parable of the unforgiving servant in Matthew 18, the first servant pleaded with the king to give him more time to pay his debt. Though he owed $10,000,000, he still had confidence, even on a servant's wages, that if there were just enough time, he could gain sufficient funds to pay it. He had no idea of his utter bankruptcy. Very possibly, this confidence in his own ability to eventually pay made him sure his fellow servant could also pay, if he just tried hard enough.

Ironically, the second servant also believed he could pay; that given enough time, he, too, could become sufficient. Neither saw their utter inability to pay the debt (to live and love perfectly), therefore neither asked for forgiveness. They just asked for more time. Their self-reliance was still untouched. As a result, both ended up in their own self-centered, self-focused prison. Hostile and isolated from each other, their earning capacity diminished even more, they were doomed to repeated and continual failure.

This describes Howard and me. Although I was a Christian and intensely following the Lord, I was still caught up in my own performance, convinced that all my striving would eventually make me acceptable. I was sure Howard could do the same. He just was not trying hard enough. More anger and more failure were always the inevitable result.

Unlove

Nancy Groom, in her book *Marriage Without Masks*, calls all such self-seeking striving "unlove." It is a hidden agenda "not to love, but to be loved."

> (We must) repent of our sinful strategies of self-protective unlove toward our spouses (but first) we must acknowledge that *our self-sufficiency is the root sin* demanding our repentance. It will be impossible to truly repent of our failure over the second commandment (to love others as ourselves) unless we first repent of our failure over the first (to love and trust God above all else). We must abandon ourselves utterly to the Father and acknowledge on a daily basis that spiritual life is found only in Him.
>
> Repentance involves two things: recognizing the sinful purpose of our lives (to stay out of pain by protecting ourselves in any way we can) and embracing a new purpose (to utterly trust God for our inner lives by dropping our self-protection and moving with openness toward our mates according to their legitimate needs). This we must do without making excuses for our failure to love....
>
> Genuine repentance admits the deep and sinful nature of our devoted commitment to self-sufficiency and, thus, does not rely on future performance to make up for the sinful self-protection of the past. We must acknowledge with unflinching candor the misdirected purposes and stubborn rootedness of our strategies for staying safe in our marriage relationships...and purpose to live increasingly without self-protection, trusting in God alone to protect our inner lives from disaster (italics added).[7]

In Dying, We Live

What is our answer, then? What do we do with this terrifying sense of insufficiency and inadequacy that has been our constant companion for so many years? Will we find our deliverance by pasting "positive self-affirmations" on the bathroom mirror, hoping that if we say them often enough we will finally believe them?

No. True freedom comes when we simply admit that we really *are* insufficient and inadequate—that we always have been, that we are now, and always will be. To quote Don Hudson from *The Silence of Adam* again, "To admit such a deficiency meant death for me." Exactly! This is precisely what God is after. God wants to bring us to the place where we will die to ourselves, to all our old ways of self-relating, self-dependence and self-sufficiency, all of which ultimately add up to self-exaltation (if I can be sufficient in myself, then I can have some of the glory).

It was this way of deliverance Jesus came to bring. "If anyone desires to come after Me, let him deny himself, and take up his cross daily, and follow Me. For whoever desires to save his life will lose it, but whoever loses his life for My sake will save it" (Luke 9:23,24).

This truth was the secret of Paul's life and ministry. "For we who live are always delivered to death for Jesus' sake, that the life of Jesus also may be manifested in our mortal flesh" (2 Cor. 4:11).

The message that tripped up Eve was not merely that she was insufficient, but also her interpretation that, as such, her condition was flawed and unacceptable.

The truth is, weakness and insufficiency are part of our design, primary components of what it means to be human. Insufficient in ourselves, we are perfectly designed to be vessels filled with God, to live and love out of His life, and thereby accomplish His purposes on earth. "We have this treasure in earthen vessels, that the excellence of the power may be of God and not of us," instructed Paul (v. 7).

Only God's life in us has ever and always been acceptable to Him. As we cease from our own striving and humbly trust all to Him, His life will be released through us. Set free from our strategies and masks, our authentic selves—who we truly are in the Lord—will begin to emerge. The automatic overflow will be the setting free of others around us. Only then can true intimacy take place. Reconciliation will follow. The fracture in the foundation of the house of the Lord will begin to mend, and the building will rise to new heights.

Truly, God is fashioning us again, male and female, into His original design.

—⁓—

Something to Think About

- Explain how we form identities (what we think about ourselves).
- What is the shame message? What part is true? What part is a lie?
- When we believe the shame message, how do we respond?

A Snare, a Fetter or a Crown?

—⚇—

I applied my heart to know, to search and seek

out wisdom and the reason of things, to know

the wickedness of folly, even of foolishness and

madness. And I find more bitter than death

the woman whose heart is snares and nets,

whose hands are fetters.

ECCLESIASTES 7:25,26

Solomon was a man who "loved the Lord, walking in the statutes of his father David" (1 Kings 3:3). His wisdom "excelled the wisdom of all the men of the East and all the wisdom of Egypt" (4:30), so that, ultimately, "King Solomon surpassed all the kings of the earth in riches and wisdom" (10:23).

Yet this amazing wisdom began when as a young, newly anointed king, he humbly beseeched God, "I am a little child; I do not know how to go out or come in. Therefore give to Your servant an understanding heart to judge Your people, that I may discern between good and evil" (3:7,9).

Solomon's request pleased God and He responded by granting great blessings:

"Behold, I have done according to your words; see, I have
given you a wise and understanding heart, so that there
has not been anyone like you before you, nor shall any
like you arise after you. And I have also given you what
you have not asked: both riches and honor, so that there
shall not be anyone like you among the kings all your
days" (vv. 12,13; see also vv. 10,11).

Solomon obviously acknowledged the God of his father, David, as
his God. At the beginning of his reign it appears his heart's desire was
to rule righteously and well. Yet several chapters later we read, "The
Lord became angry with Solomon, because his heart had turned from
the Lord God of Israel." So angry was God that He announced, "I will
surely tear the kingdom away from you" (1 Kings 11:9,11).

How could it be that such a humble, wise beginning went so horribly awry?

The Influence of Women

But King Solomon loved many foreign [idolatrous]
women,....from the nations of whom the Lord had said to
the children of Israel, "You shall not intermarry with
them, nor they with you. Surely they will turn away your
hearts after their gods." Solomon clung to these in love.
[H]is wives turned his heart after other gods; and his heart
was not loyal to the Lord his God" (vv. 1,2,4).

Herbert Lockyer, author of *All the Women of the Bible*, observes,

No man has ever lived who has had as much experience
with women as King Solomon, who "loved many strange
women." Having 700 wives, princesses, and 300 concu-
bines, all of whom it would seem were idolaters, we can
readily understand how they turned away his heart from
God. It was because of Solomon's gross adultery and idolatry that the kingdom he had raised to illustrious heights
was so tragically rent in twain. It is not surprising, then,

that Solomon has as much to say about both the vices and virtues of women as he does in the book of Proverbs.[1]

King Solomon, the wisest man in the world, was brought to spiritual ruin by his marriages to idolatrous women. He had other sins, but we are told it was this sin, his love for ungodly women, that turned his heart from the Lord.

The book of Proverbs makes it abundantly clear that God has given woman a place of incredible influence. She was called a "help" from her beginning and, as such, the man was instructed to "cleave" to her.

God intended her influence to be felt, but God was after influence for "good and not evil" (Prov. 31:12). She was to be a help "as to the Lord" (Eph. 5:22). Yet here again we can see the ravages of Satan's evil plan all around us.

Good or Evil?

What is good? Good is what proceeds from God. Evil is anything that proceeds from another source, no matter how "good" it looks. Its ultimate end is death.

In chapter 3, I stated, "As the first sin was, so shall all the sins afterwards be...in every sin we can see 'self' at work....Self is God's greatest enemy."

A woman who influences for evil may not necessarily fit the picture of those we would normally describe as evil. She may not be one we would consider "morally loose." She might not drink, smoke, sleep around or spend foolishly. She may simply be one who is dedicated to her own needs, her own way and the satisfaction of her own ego. This self-devotion will profoundly affect the way she relates to men because she will seek them for selfish purposes, to advance her own agenda (what we have earlier called "the desire of the woman"). This self-centeredness is a form of idolatry; it is actually "self-idolatry" or "self-worship." God calls it "evil."

Solomon describes this kind of woman in our opening Scripture (Eccles. 7:25,26):

I applied my heart to know, to search and seek out wis-

dom and the reason of things, to know the wickedness of
folly, even of foolishness and madness. And I find more
bitter than death the woman whose heart is snares and
nets, whose hands are fetters.

As Solomon applied his heart to seek wisdom, his understanding
grew more clear, and with the clarity came a deep grief he likens to the
"bitterness of death." He declared that the heart of an evil woman is
"like snares and nets and her hands are as bands or fetters" for the one
lured into her lair. Herbert Lockyer says in *All the Women of the
Bible*, Solomon saw that the women who had enticed him from God
were "more bitter than death."[2]

Solomon knew firsthand the truth stated in Proverbs 6:32, that a
man entering into an adulterous relationship "lacks understanding;...so
destroys his own soul." This may not mean that Solomon lost his place
in eternity, but it does mean that his effectiveness here on earth, especially as it relates to God's kingdom, was greatly diminished.

The Evil Woman

What defines an evil woman? In Scripture she is called a "harlot." In
God's eyes, harlotry is not limited to sexual promiscuity. It is symbolic of spiritual adultery, someone whose heart is turned from God and
seeks satisfaction apart from His life and ways. Some of the characteristics of such a woman are listed in Proverbs as follows:

- She is a woman who flatters with her words to ensure her
  own agenda is met (see 7:21).
- She uses sex to manipulate and attract the man (see vv. 16-18).
- She depends on her physical appearance (clothing) to
  attract, but has a "crafty (subtle, hidden, concealed)[3] heart"
  (see v. 10). (She gives her body, but keeps her heart hidden
  and concealed.)
- She is "loud and rebellious, her feet would not stay at home"
  (v. 11).
- When her husband is not "at home" (we could interpret
  this physically, emotionally or spiritually), she looks to

other "lovers" (people, methods or strategies) to satisfy her desires (see vv. 18,19).

- "Her ways are unstable" so she cannot be known (5:6).

She does all this to accomplish her own ends, to satisfy her own need to establish "self" worth (the wrong kind), to be loved, found acceptable and desirable. This is the woman who influences for evil.

The Godly Woman

If you are like me, as you read the previous list, your mind immediately raced to the woman mentioned in 1 Peter 3, whom we described earlier in the book. These characteristics are in direct opposition to the behavior Peter encourages for the godly woman. Based on what we learned about the godly woman in Proverbs 7, what can we say about her here?

- She is a woman who is responsible with her words. She neither flatters insincerely, or cuts vengefully with her words. She speaks the truth in love (see 1 Pet. 3:1).
- She does not depend on her attire (sex appeal) to attract or manipulate the man (see v. 3).
- She is not hidden and concealed of heart, rather she is *adorned* with "the hidden person of the heart." She accompanies her sexual intimacy with emotional intimacy. She does not withhold sex to "punish" her husband, and she does not engage in sex to "appease" her husband. Trusting God, she presses through her fear of rejection and works at resolving the real issues in their life (see vv. 4-6).
- Rather than being loud and rebellious, running here and there, her heart is engaged with her husband and family. She is gentle and appropriately submissive to her own husband, knowing that their destiny is together (see vv. 1,4,7).
- She sees beyond her own desires for self-gratification to God's plan and purpose for her as a woman. Even when disappointed, she seeks God's strength and love to continue to invest in her husband and children (see vv. 1-6).
- The opposite of unstable, she is steadfast, undisturbed,

"quiet"[4] of spirit. She knows who she is in the Lord; therefore she is able to be known by others (see vv. 4,5).

This is the woman who influences for good. Her willingness to be
open and honest with her husband (to be adorned with the hidden
person of the heart) is, in the sight of God, "very precious." This
woman's help is "unto the Lord" to advance His kingdom, not her own.

Too Soon Old, Too Late Smart

We can only wonder if Solomon (the writer of Proverbs 31) learned the
lessons King Lemuel learned from his mother. If he did learn them, he

—⟪⟫—

The virtuous woman's value is said to be far
above the preciousness of rubies.

—⟪⟫—

learned them too late. Consider the description of a virtuous woman
found in Proverbs 31. We will discuss only a few of them here:
"Who can find a virtuous wife?
For her worth is far above rubies" (v. 10).
This verse tells us that the worth of such a woman is greater than
anything we would place value on in this life. Precious gems and met-
als are one of the ways the world measures wealth. The virtuous
woman's value is said to be far above the preciousness of rubies.
"The heart of her husband safely trusts her;
So he will have no lack of gain" (v. 11).
What a tremendous statement in relation to the blessedness of this
union. Scripture frequently speaks of putting our trust solely in God:
"Trust in Him [the Lord] at all times, you people; pour out your heart
before Him; God is a refuge for us" (Ps. 62:8).
Yet here in Proverbs we are told that a man who has found a godly
wife can also safely trust his heart to her. "Safely trust" means "to run
to for refuge, to be confident and sure or secure, a place of safety."[5]

As we have already noted, the heart denotes "thoughts, feelings, mind, middle." It is the deepest, most inner recess of ourselves, the place where the real person dwells. A woman who has found her worth, purpose and security in Christ, will become a safe haven for her husband as he makes the same journey. Embracing and sharing her own insufficiency, she can free her husband to own his. He will not be afraid to tell her of his fears of weakness and failure.

Bringing these things out into the light will be a major healing step, a critical unmasking of the enemy's lies in his life that will have far-reaching effects. Other relationships will be profoundly affected by his newfound freedom. One wife whose husband had made great strides on this journey to wholeness said,

> [As we talked through the months] we discovered that there were things from my husband's childhood that had shaped his opinion of himself and thus affected his behavior all through his life. As he shared these experiences with me, they released their hold on him and true healing took place. Eventually he was able to leave those years behind forever....
>
> Ultimately a new maturity began to emerge in him that has affected every aspect of his life. Not only our relationship, but others, the children, business associates and social contacts have all benefited by his new ability to face life head on. The principles he learned about being honest in our relationship were principles for living that overflowed into every other area of his life.[6]

This kind of emotional intimacy is what our Father God had in mind for His children. It is recorded of the first couple in the garden: "And they were both naked, the man and his wife, and were not ashamed" (Gen. 2:25). Surely, this is symbolic of the emotional openness God intended for us. Within the walls of this trusting framework we reach our full potential and "lack no gain" as we grow together in our discovery of God's wonderful provision for us.

"She does him good and not evil
All the days of her life" (Prov. 31:12).

This is a woman who has her husband's highest good always in mind.

(Some have said this is the definition of "agape" love, God's kind of love.)

What is good in the sight of God? It is that which draws Godward. This does not mean the godly woman is "religious," always quoting Scripture to teach or prove her point. Rather, like the woman in 1 Peter 3, she lives her life from scriptural principles through the power of the Holy Spirit. In the normal give-and-take of daily life, by her own behavior and responsible words, she demonstrates God's heart.

"She opens her mouth with wisdom,
And on her tongue is the law of kindness.
She watches over the ways of her household" (vv. 26,27).

The word "watches" in these verses is the same Hebrew word *tsaphah* translated "watchman" in other places in Scripture. A good example is Ezekiel 3:17, which states, "Son of man, I have made you a watchman for the house of Israel; therefore hear a word from My mouth, and give them warning from Me."

—⧕—

[A woman's] activities include not only the physical care of the home, but she is also a "watchman" over the emotional and spiritual condition of her family.

—⧕—

The *Spirit-Filled Life Bible* informs us: "In ancient Israel watchmen were stationed on the walls to warn people of danger and the approach of messengers."[7]

Teachings about the virtuous woman in Proverbs 31 often focus only on a description of her physical labor and financial prowess. I think there is strong scriptural evidence, however, that much of the activity in these verses can be interpreted in a spiritual manner. As we consider the woman who "looketh well" to the ways of her household (as the *King James Version* renders it) or "watches over" the ways of her house, instinctively our thoughts can be limited to her many household tasks. This word *tsaphah*, though, tells us that her role moves far beyond the joys of making a home. Her activities include not only the physical care of the home, but she is also a "watchman" over the emotional and spiritual condition of her family. The following verses beautifully describe her spiritual activity:

"She seeks wool and flax,
And willingly works with her hands" (Prov. 31:13).

Here we see the hands of blessing rather than the hands that snare, entice and destroy. These are hands that bring life, hands that will seek out a "far Kingdom" and work to bring the reality of that Kingdom to her household.

The godly woman works willingly with her hands to provide coverings of wool and flax. Wool covers from the cold. Sometimes cold, in Scripture, is symbolic of God's judgment against sin. For example:

> He gives snow like wool; He scatters the frost like ashes; He casts out His hail like morsels; who can stand before His cold? (Ps. 147:16,17).

Similarly, wool can cover from such judgment, as we can see from the following Scripture:

> Therefore I will return and take away My grain in its time and My new wine in its season, and I will take back My wool and My linen [flax], given to cover her nakedness (Hos. 2:9).

Scarlet wool and hyssop dipped in blood were used in the Old Testament ceremonies to cleanse God's people from sin (see Heb. 9:19-22). Symbolically, flax, or linen, refers to Christ's righteousness for the saints.

The woman's hands mentioned here are *kaph* hands, which refers to hands opened or upturned, and can refer to hands extended in prayer (see Exod. 9:29 and Isa. 1:15),[8] beseeching God on behalf of those in her household. The woman is appealing to God's mercy and grace. She is seeking wool from God, wool that covers and protects her family from the judgment of sin, and flax that they may be clothed in Christ's righteousness.

She knows the God of Moses who said, "[I am] merciful and gracious, longsuffering, and abounding in goodness and truth, keeping mercy for thousands [a thousand generations of those who love me], forgiving iniquity and transgression and sin" (Exod. 34:6,7; see also 20:6).

Moses was so taken by God's description of Himself that even though the people for whom he was interceding had sinned a great sin, he immediately appealed to what God had just told him and said, "[E]ven though we are a stiff-necked people;...pardon our iniquity and our sin, and take us as Your inheritance" (Exod. 34:9). God quickly responded affirmatively making a promise to perform great miracles on their behalf (see v. 10).

The virtuous woman knows that God is just waiting for people to intercede for their loved ones so He can show them favor and move on their behalf. She knows that He looks for those who will "stand in the gap...that [He] should not destroy" (Ezek. 22:30). Therefore, with confidence it is written of her, "She is not afraid of snow [or cold] for her household, for all her household is clothed [covered] with scarlet [symbolic of the blood of Christ]" (Prov. 31:21). She knows her very purpose is to be a worker together with God to bring forth the kingdom of God and His righteousness in her family.

"She is like the merchant ships,
She brings her food from afar" (v. 14).

This woman imports "food" for her family—not only physical food, but also more importantly, "spiritual" food. This is food that comes from a "far country."

A merchant ship transfers goods from one place to another. The virtuous woman is likened to such a ship. She, too, brings or transfers goods from one place to another.

She brings her food from afar. In her prayers and meditation on the Word, as she watches and waits upon the Lord, she travels to a far country—to the kingdom of God. There she partakes of "the bread of life." As God begins to nourish her and bring her into the ways of the kingdom, "she perceives [tastes] that her merchandise is good" (v. 18). Her own heart, radically transformed, becomes a "merchant ship," a vehicle that God uses to bring that same bread of life to her family. Some in the house may yet be apathetic or hostile to God, but even they will be fed by the changed life of the virtuous woman as she lives out the principles of the kingdom before them.

"Strength and honor are her clothing;
She shall rejoice in time to come" (v. 25).

The word "strength" comes from a verb that means to be stout, to prevail, to be strong, to harden against the enemy.[9] The *Theological Wordbook of the Old Testament* tells us this word means "strength, might, particularly of warriors."[10] (We'll cover this aspect of the virtuous woman more thoroughly in the next chapter.)

"She rejoices [laughs in derision][11] over the future [the latter day or time to come, knowing that she and her family are in readiness for it]" (v. 25, *Amp.*). This woman's position is strong and secure; her strength and security are in God. She is confident of the future because she is confident in the God of the future to whom she has committed all things. She has come to know Him intimately. As a result, she trusts Him implicitly. Her rest is based solely in Him.

Psalm 2:4 uses this same word for laugh when it says that "[God] who sits in the heavens shall laugh;...hold...in derision" the kings and rulers that "take counsel together, against the Lord and against His Anointed" (v. 2). The anointed are the family of God. Although the word "anointed" is capitalized here, it also refers to Christ's Body, the anointed on earth.

God laughs! He laughs at the plans of the enemy for our lives, for our families' lives. Because God laughs at the plans of the enemy—plans for the destruction, pain and defeat he has plotted for our lives—we, too, can laugh. Satan is a defeated foe. Christ has won the victory. He has been seated at the right hand of the Father in heavenly places. He is "far above all principality and power and might and dominion, and every name that is named, not only in this age but also in that which is to come. And He has put all things under His feet" (Eph. 1:21,22). This is why He can laugh!

"And you He made alive, and raised us up together, and made us sit together in the heavenly places in Christ Jesus" (2:1,6). This is why we, too, can laugh! The godly woman knows this, and she is unafraid for herself and her family "in the time to come."

A Snare, a Fetter or a Crown?

A virtuous woman is a crown to her husband: but she that maketh ashamed is as rottenness in his bones (Prov. 12:4, *KJV*).

If we were going to sum up what we have said about the "evil woman," one "whose heart is snares and nets and whose hands are fetters," we could say that she is one who makes her husband "ashamed." She does him evil, not good. She is as "rottenness" in his bones.

Bones can allude to strength in Scripture,[12] and rottenness means to decay or erode. A woman who brings shame to her husband erodes his strength. It will be extremely difficult for him to become the man God intended him to be. Solomon's life was a vivid example of this kind of erosion of strength and character.

A virtuous woman, however, the godly woman described in Proverbs 31, is a "crown to her husband." What does this mean?

Crowns relate to wisdom. Wisdom, we are told in Proverbs 4:8,9, will "bring you honor, when you embrace her. She will place on your head an ornament of grace; a crown of glory she will deliver to you."

A crown encircles the head. The word "crown" is taken from a word that means "to encircle (for attack or protection)."[13] So the basic meaning here is much like the word for "help" in Genesis 2:18, which is "to surround and protect."

Wisdom, when embraced, when received to oneself, brings great honor because it helps one to walk uprightly, to make good decisions, to have a healthy mental attitude and, most importantly, creates a right attitude toward God. Wisdom, in effect, surrounds and protects the mind, and brings great honor to the "head" of one who has it. It is like a crown.

So, also, is the godly woman, in whose mouth is wisdom and kindness (see Prov. 31:26). When embraced, when received by the man as the help God has given, she, too, will be instrumental in surrounding and protecting the man's mind. It is significant that the heart (which the man can safely trust to a virtuous wife) is alternately translated as "understanding."[14]

God has uniquely and specifically designed the woman to influence her husband's understanding more profoundly than any other person in his life. The physical intimacy God intended to be unique to marriage is a powerful agent that can move the man to deep emotional intimacy. As he opens to his wife, she will draw him out, into the light of true relationship. As he walks with her in truth and vulnerability, she will help him to sort mentally and emotionally, to make good decisions, help bring him into godly balance. She will bring him honor: "a crown."

Although the Proverbs woman is obviously a leader in her own right, it says of her husband that he "is known in the gates, when he sits among the elders of the land" (v. 23). "It was a great honor to sit among the elders at the gates."[15] The leaders of the city sat there. This woman's husband not only sits among the elders, but he is also renowned among them; he is recognized and known as one who has significant wisdom.

A leader in God's kingdom is not necessarily one who physically stands in front and has a public ministry. "Whoever desires to become great among you shall be your servant," Jesus declared in Mark 10:43. Leadership takes many forms. Whatever a man's ministry or vocation, his abilities will be greatly enhanced by the influence of a godly woman. Instead of "rottenness," she will be a strength to his bones; she will help build his character with far-reaching effects.

Ultimately, though it may take some time, the faithful, godly woman will experience the joy of God's promise:

> Her children [will] rise up and bless her; her husband also, and he praises her, saying: "Many daughters have done nobly, but you excel them all." Charm is deceitful and beauty is vain [empty, transitory], but a woman who fears the Lord, she shall be praised (Prov. 31:28-30, *NASB*).

I am personally staggered and greatly humbled by God's plan for the woman He has formed for Himself. It is an awesome responsibility, a great privilege in the Lord. The honor and influence God has given to women is almost beyond comprehension. No wonder the enemy has fought through the centuries to quiet her, to denigrate her, to steal from God and the man that which God designed to bring him honor and strength.

Will you take your mantle, women? Will you become the crown God designed you to be? Will you receive them, men, to your own welfare? The state of the Church lies in our hands.

—⁂—

Something to Think About

- What are some characteristics of an evil woman? What are some characteristics of a godly woman?

- Explain what it is about the virtuous woman that will cause her husband to safely trust his heart to her.
- Describe what it means for a woman to be a crown to her husband.

The Warrior Woman

—*&*—

"And I will put enmity between you and the woman,
and between your seed and her Seed; He shall
bruise your head, and you shall bruise His heel."

GENESIS 3:15

God speaks. He speaks of the future, of restoration—a promise of deliverance. Despite catastrophic failure, despite deception and betrayal, when all would seem to be over, ruined, beyond repair, God speaks of recovery. His first words of promise specifically concern the woman.

In the opening passage God is addressing Satan, who had made his first inroad by deceiving Eve. God is telling him that he has not won. Satan's demise will yet come, and it will come through the seed of the very one he had so craftily beguiled—the woman.

Right from the beginning God operates true to form, true to the nature of His heart. Again and again, in life and in Scripture, we see the redemptive, restorative and victorious hand of God as He comes back to strategic points of conflict, places of seeming defeat, where Satan has attempted to turn good into evil, and life into death. At that exact point God brings triumph out of the devastation. He doesn't stop there, though. He uses the very conflict to teach and strengthen His own so they then become formidable foes of the enemy, in battling for themselves and others. Such is the case with Eve. "In the net which they [Satan] hid, their [his] own foot is caught" (Ps. 9:15).

The Enmity of the Woman

Eve was the first on earth to be ensnared by Satan's cunning deceitfulness. She was also the first to expose these very traits in him, calling him what he was—a deceiver. "The serpent deceived me, and I ate" (Gen. 3:13). God immediately passed sentence, and He began where the sin began, with the serpent: "You are cursed more than all cattle, and more than every beast of the field; on your belly you shall go, and you shall eat dust all the days of your life" (v. 14).

God then continues with our opening Scripture: "I will put enmity [hostility, antagonism] between you and the woman" (v. 15). What a powerful statement, and how often it is overlooked! God is specifically speaking of the woman here, not of humanity as a whole. Let the effect of what God is saying sink into your spirit. God was telling Satan that not only would he (Satan) be woman's enemy, but also that more importantly, God was making woman Satan's enemy! The *American Heritage Dictionary* defines enmity as "deep seated, often mutual hatred."[1]

By Eve's exposure of Satan, an enmity was now created between them that God is saying would continue down through the ages. Women who are turned wholly to God would be used in some very direct and devastating ways to expose Satan's tactics and come against his kingdom.

The Seed of the Woman

Our Scripture verse goes on to declare that the enmity would also be between "your [Satan's] seed and her Seed; He shall bruise your head, and you shall bruise His heel" (v. 15).

The earth had been made for humanity to rule. "The heaven...the Eternal holds himself, the earth he has assigned to men" (Ps. 115:16, *Moffatt Translation*). "God didn't give away ownership of the earth," declares Dutch Sheets in *Intercessory Prayer*, "but He did assign the responsibility of governing it to humanity."[2]

We know, though, that humanity fell. They would continue to govern, but under a different authority. Paul Billheimer in *Destined to*

Overcome, says that when Adam "transferred his allegiance from God to Satan, he also transferred his dominion."[3] The earth would be governed by a new "head," Satan himself. The one who had declared his intent from the beginning, that of self-exaltation over God, had won the first skirmish. Satan would now be "ruler of this world" (John 12:31). God, however, announced right up front that Satan's "headship" was temporary at best. The One in the wings would wrest it away from him—the Seed of the woman.

God would not allow Satan or the woman to move from that place without the promise of restoration fully declared. Eve was the first to be ensnared by Satan, but she was also the first to expose his true nature. She was also the subject of the first promise of deliverance. Through the Seed of the woman "[sin and] death [would be] swallowed up in victory" (1 Cor. 15:54). Through the Seed of the woman God would "[disarm] principalities and powers, [making] a public spectacle of them, triumphing over them in it" (Col. 2:15). Heaven and earth's greatest victory would be realized out of the greatest point of defeat.

The Authority Returned

When Jesus, the perfect Seed, came forth through woman, and the Seed went down into death, it looked as though Satan had won again. Acts 2:24, however, says, "God raised Him up, liberating Him from the pangs of death, seeing that it was not possible for Him to continue to be controlled or retained by it" *(Amp.).* "In Him was life" (John 1:4). It was not possible for the grave to hold Him. "I am He who lives, and was dead, and behold, I am alive forevermore....And I have the keys of Hades [hell] and of Death," Jesus declared to John in Revelation 1:18. Jesus had come forth from death victoriously, bringing with Him the legal right for humanity to rule again.

Jesus, the perfect, sinless man, had bruised the head of Satan, and leveled a death blow to his authority. As a man, and on behalf of humanity, Jesus had taken back the headship under God that Adam had lost, and returned it forever to every believer who would come under His Lordship. However, as in the beginning, there would be work to do.

It is important to note that when Jesus defeated Satan, He did not annihilate him. From humanity's inception, God declared that part of their dominion over the earth would be to "subdue" (war against and tread underfoot) any hostile force that would raise itself up against the plans and purposes of God. This is still the believer's calling.

Satan is a defeated foe, but God is raising up a Church, a Bride "meet" (suitable) for, and corresponding to her Bridegroom. This "raising up" entails a learning to war, an entering into battle to "possess the kingdom" we have already been given, a growing to maturity as we walk in His authority.[4] Satan has been left on earth that, through the conflict, the Church might be *strengthened*, not defeated, and he will remain only as long as he serves God's purposes.

—⁓—

Although both men and women are critically important to God's plan to exercise His will on earth, He has uniquely designed women to move into this battle.

—⁓—

Christ's victory over Satan was not won for Himself. It was to return to humanity the authority they had lost. Christ's purposes will not be fulfilled until the Church is fully enforcing His victory.

The Strength of an Army

Enter (again) the "virtuous woman." Although both men and women are critically important to God's plan to exercise His will on earth, He has uniquely designed women to move into this battle, as we shall soon discover.

Often when we think of the virtuous woman we think of piety and moral purity. Although these qualities would certainly be included in such a woman, the Hebrew meaning of this word goes far beyond the description of character traits.

Chayil is the Hebrew word for virtuous. It means "force, whether of men, means, or other resources [God!]." It also means "strength, able, might, power," and is used to describe the strength of an army.' In l Chronicles 5:18, men of war were called *chayil* men, valiant men, men of great strength. Intriguingly, it shares the same consonantal root as the word that means "to twist or whirl, writhe in pain as in childbirth, bear or bring forth."[6]

What an interesting combination of words to describe a woman God calls virtuous! He is telling us that she is a warrior woman who also knows about bringing something to birth—and she is Satan's enemy!

Warring Hands

Proverbs 14:1 states that a "wise woman builds her house [or family], but the foolish [perverse] pulls it down with her hands." Here again we see the use of the woman's hands—for good or for evil. She has the power to build (make or repair)[7] her house with her hands and she has the power destroy it.

Two kinds of hands are mentioned in Proverbs 31. We mentioned *kaph* hands in the last chapter; we saw that they are stretched-out hands, beseeching God for His grace and mercy upon families. Another kind of hands, though, is spoken of here—*yad* hands. These are hands that may be "open or closed in a grasp or fist."[8] *Yad* hands can indicate "power, means, direction."[9] The woman uses both kinds of hands to help build her house.

Psalm 144:1 says, "[He] trains my hands [*yad*] for war, and my fingers for battle." (Fingers denote "grasping, something to seize with.")[10] The virtuous woman has learned to "war or battle" in the spirit realm. She has developed "warring hands."

As a woman whose heart is turned to God, she has begun to see things from His perspective, from His eternal outlook. Because her center has been turned, she no longer relates all to herself (she is no longer "perverse" or "foolish"). Rather, she has become a worker together with God for fulfilling His purpose and plan on earth specifically as it relates to her household—her husband and children.

The virtuous woman has moved out of a "man-centered" or "self-centered" emphasis into a "God-centered" emphasis. DeVern Fromke writes,

As believers God is either the center of our universe and

we have become rightly adjusted to Him, or we have made ourselves the center and are attempting to make all else orbit around us and for us. When the center is wrong then everything in our reckoning is wrong.[11]

Once our centers have been turned God-ward, we become exceedingly threatening to the enemy. God begins to reveal His heart to those thus turned. "The secret of the Lord is with those who fear Him, and He will show them His covenant" (Ps. 25:14). He will reveal His covenant—sealed with the blood of the Lamb slain from the foundation of the earth—to our hearts. This is the Abrahamic covenant, the promise of blessing, multiplication and victory over our enemies. It is the promise of the restoration and fulfillment of everything God planned for His children from the foundation of the world (see Gen. 12:13; 22:17,18; Rom. 4:3; Gal. 3:9,14). It is the return of our authority in Jesus Christ to rule and reign in the spiritual realm in His name.

Having moved out of ourselves into a new relationship with God, He is now able to move, speak and act through us to silence and drive back the enemy as we learn what it is to "walk in the Spirit" (see Rom. 8:1). As we "submit to God" [first and foremost] [and then] "Resist the devil," we are promised that he will "flee" [run away] from us (Jas. 4:7). We will become his enemy!

Satan, even though it galls him, will say of us as was said of Israel when they left behind 40 years of wilderness wandering (symbolic of the self-life) where everyone did "whatever is right in his own eyes" (Deut. 12:8). As they prepared to cross Jordan in order to possess the Promised Land, the Canaanites were terrified. They had already heard of the incredible, awesome power of Israel's God who fought for them in battle and defeated every enemy. Rahab, a citizen of Canaan, said, "I know that the Lord has given you the land, that the terror of you has fallen on us, and that all the inhabitants of the land are fainthearted because of you" (Josh. 2:9).

So shall Satan and his minions say of us, for we, too, have crossed Jordan; we have left the self-life behind to walk in the Spirit. Satan has been dreading this day. We are now ready to "build our house" (the House of the Lord, our own and corporately) according to God's blueprint and by His power. "Unless the Lord builds the house, they labor in vain who build it" (Ps. 127:1). As we truly represent God's heart, we will truly wield God's authority.

She Shall Rejoice in Time to Come

As stated in our previous chapter, the word "rejoice" means "to laugh or hold in derision, contempt or scorn." It also means to "mock or ridicule."

—⚬⚬—

When a woman becomes "virtuous," one who has been awakened to her womanhood as God purposed it from the beginning, the end is near for the arch deceiver in her life.

—⚬⚬—

Who is it the woman will hold in contempt or scorn but the very one to whom God said she would be an enemy? Satan, of course!

We are in the habit of referring to Satan as our enemy when in reality, according to God, the exact opposite is true. God has set us, particularly as women, to be Satan's enemy. By exposing him in the temptation, Eve chose to make the breach, and God Himself widened it, declaring that it would continue down through the ages.

This enmity, this hatred between the two of them, explains Satan's attack on woman throughout the centuries. Knowing that she was created to be man's help, Satan also knew that if she was ever restored to her rightful position, he would be greatly hindered in his ability to continue to bring confusion and distortion to homes and families. By deceiving the woman, his hope was to undermine or weaken all of God's plan. His attack on her has continued for the same reason.

How is it that Satan comes against woman? He twists and distorts her role, her place in God's plan. Knowing that God has made her especially sensitive to the devil's activity, that God has put a "hatred" into her heart against him, Satan works continually to silence her and render her powerless and useless.

Throughout the centuries, Satan has caused woman to be used, abused and subverted; and even in the best of circles, woman is often considered not quite worthy of genuine consideration. By minimizing, devaluing or objectifying the woman in the eyes of man, he knows her words will not be taken seriously, and the one who would expose his works is rendered ineffective again. His time, however, is limited. Woman will yet have "the last laugh."

Eyes to See

Satan's tactics will work only as long as the woman herself is blind to her role and to the power God has given her to fulfill it. When a woman becomes "virtuous," one who has been awakened to her womanhood as God purposed it from the beginning, the end is near for the arch deceiver in her life. John 8:32 declares that when we come to "know the truth," when we come into an intimate, personal, revelation knowledge of God's heart, character, ways, the reality of who He is, "the truth shall make [us] free."

This personal knowledge of God's heart will begin to impart a strength and a confidence in the virtuous woman that is not of herself. She begins to understand the spirit realm. Her perspective changes; she sees and understands the issues she faces in a clearer, sharper way.

"The fear of the Lord is the beginning of wisdom," declares Proverbs 9:10. Coming into relationship with the Almighty, the Creator of the universe, is the beginning place of wisdom and understanding. Proverbs tells us that all else—human thinking, human strategizing, human ways, when not submitted to God—are foolishness.

The prayer of Paul in Ephesians 1:17-23 is a universal prayer God would have us pray today. God wants us to ask for the "spirit of wisdom and revelation" that only comes through "the knowledge of Him." The accurate knowledge of God will open "the eyes of [our] understanding." We will come to truly know and comprehend the fullness of what Christ has bought back for us, and "what is the exceeding greatness of His power toward us who believe." This is the same power that raised Jesus victorious from the grave, and then seated Him in heavenly places, far above all principality, all power, all might, all dominion and every name that is named, not only in this age, but also in the age which is to come, and put "all things under His feet." Not just a few things, not even most things, but *all* things were put under His feet!

Ephesians 2:5,6 declares that we, too, were raised up with Him by that same power from our dead, helpless state, and were seated with Him in the same heavenly places. This power is resurrection power! It brings life out of death. This unfailing, undefeatable, eternal power, God says works toward us, in us and through us if we believe (see Acts 3:12; Eph. 3:20). Now that is victory power!

The virtuous woman is one who has come into an intimate relationship with God. She knows Him in the Spirit. She knows His heart. She knows what He is about. She understands the covenant. The "eyes of her understanding" are opened, and she now begins to move in a realm of spiritual authority that is powerful. She takes her place as a "watchman" for God, who "watches over the ways of her household" (Prov. 31:27). She sees the enemy's tactics as he comes against her family members in his endeavor to keep them from moving into God's destiny for them, and she knows the power she has against him.

Partaking now of the tree of life—the life of God—His life is surging through her. The enemy is no longer "safe." She puts on God's armor and "girdeth her loins with strength, and strengtheneth her arms" (v. 17, *KJV*) for the battle. Not only has she become a worker together with God, but she is also walking in a new awareness that she has heaven's help to bring to birth heaven's plan for building her household.

She will be used to pull down principalities and to push back the forces of darkness. She will seize, grasp, take back that which was stolen by the enemy and call forth those things that "do not exist as though they did" (Rom. 4:17). The Holy Spirit has taught her hands to war!

The Travailing Woman

Earlier we noted related Hebrew words for "virtue": "strength, might" and "twisting, a writhing in pain as in childbirth, to bear or bring forth." We have also stated that God designed woman—physically, emotionally and spiritually—in a way that would equip her to "help" the man.

God chose to write within the nature of woman an innate desire to bring forth life. She understands she will go through a time of difficulty, body changes, morning (and sometimes "all day") sickness. Ultimately, she will go through the pain of labor and delivery before that life is brought forth. Yet, because of her deep desire for life, she gives herself to this process with joy and anticipation. Thousands, perhaps millions, of dollars have been spent in the United States alone by infertile women desiring to give birth.

This desire does not always surface right away. I remember my own daughter, as a young woman approaching the age of marriage, saying she did not want to have children. She had spent her early teen years baby-sitting, and had grown weary of caring for small children. She was sure that life with a husband would be all the enjoyment she would need. Sure enough, though, not too long after marriage, I began to see this innate yearning of a woman begin to stir within her. She would linger at the racks of baby clothes in the mall, notice babies as their mothers strolled them by, talk about "cute names." Not long after she announced, "We're pregnant!" God Himself put the desire to reproduce in the hearts of humanity, but especially so in the hearts of women. This is also true in the spiritual realm.

Spiritual Reproduction

As I travel and speak to people around the world, I make it a point to talk about the "circle" of prayer as often as I can. I have discovered that all biblical truth runs in a circular fashion. It begins in heaven with the will, the heart, the plan and the purpose of God. He then looks for those on earth who have ears to hear and eyes to see by the Spirit what He is saying and wanting to do. As they begin to sense what is on God's heart in a given situation, whether it be in a family, a city or a nation, it becomes "implanted" in the womb of their spirit where it continues to grow through the watering of the Word and confirmation of others. When the fullness of time has come—when God is ready to fulfill that word—a deep inner knowing takes place. There begins a labor or a travail within the person's spirit that will ultimately cause the will of God to break forth in the earth. It then flows back to heaven, fulfilled as God purposed.

Jesus instructed us to pray, "Our Father...Thy kingdom come, Thy will be done in earth, as it is in heaven" (Matt. 6:9,10, *KJV*). Prayer has always been about God's will being accomplished. In relationship with our Father, our privilege is bringing that will to earth. This has been our intended birthright from the beginning.

Prayer is not something we do to try to force God's hand, to try to convince Him to do something He does not want to do. It is spending time with Him, getting to know Him, and as a result, we begin to perceive what is really on His heart. We discover that He is a good God, that what He wants for His children is better than anything we have ever imagined. We then begin to pronounce His Word—His will—on earth. Because it is His Word, we stand in His authority against every force that would attempt to hinder it from coming forth. We resist the enemy. He must flee, and God's kingdom comes to earth through our labor, travail and warfare.

How well I remember the awakening in my own life as I began to become aware of God's plan for me as a "virtuous woman." My marriage was floundering, and I had a son who had become addicted to drugs and alcohol. I felt powerless to make any kind of a meaningful difference. At times I felt like a helpless observer standing on the shore of a great body of water that was about to engulf the lives of those I loved, and I was unable to reach them.

In my great impotence God began to teach me. I began to discover the reality of who God has called me to be as a woman, as His daughter. A strength began to flow into me that was different from anything I had ever experienced. It wasn't "pulling myself up by the bootstraps." It wasn't "self-talk," trying to convince myself that "someday" things would probably work out by themselves.

I realized I was in a war! This war was not about me. It was about God's awesome plan unfolding on earth, and the knowledge that God intended for every member of my household to come into the fullness of His kingdom. This was not a battle I would fight by myself or in my own strength. God Himself was resident in me to help.

He revealed the battle plan and the weapons of warfare He had secured for me in Jesus Christ. I began to understand what it means to be dressed in "clothing [of] fine linen and purple" (Prov. 31:22), the clothing of priests and kings.[12] As a priest, I have entrance by the Spirit into the "Holiest of All," into the very sanctuary and presence of God Himself, to intercede for my loved ones (see Heb. 10:19,20). Having been seated with Christ, the King of kings, I have His authority in the heavenly realm to move against principalities and powers and everything that would lift itself up against the purposes of God in my family.

God spoke strength to my once fainting heart: "The victory is assured!" As surely as He spoke to the Israelites when they embarked upon the possession of the land God had promised them, He said to me, "Fear not, don't be discouraged, don't be dismayed. I have given you the land. Every place where you plant your foot I have already given you. Just begin to walk and war" (see Josh. 1:3,6-9). It was as though steel came into my backbone!

I remember the day when I said to the enemy, "You have gone this far, you will go no farther!" The enemy knows when we mean business. He knows when we know the truth! He knows when he has been found out, that he has been defeated and that he has no power to keep people in bondage any longer.

That day I gave God permission to do whatever He had to do to bring forth His kingdom in my household. I was ready to "build." God had just been waiting to hear those words. He loves desperate prayers—and I was a desperate woman!

As I began to "war" and "bring to birth," my prayers had many different kinds of expressions. There was everything from weeping to laughing, from praising to warring, to just confidently "standing," knowing the victory had been won even before I saw the results with my natural eyes.

Jesus assures us, "Whatever you ask in My name, that I will do, that the Father may be glorified in the Son." Then, just in case we can't seem to believe such an incredible promise, He immediately repeats it: "If you ask anything in My name, I will do it" (John 14:13,14). His purpose is that "the Father may be glorified in the Son." This is for *Him!* It is what *He* wants!

Again, in John 15:7,8, Jesus declares, "If you abide in Me, and My words abide in you, you will ask what you desire, and it shall be done for you. By this My Father is glorified, that you bear much fruit; so you will be My disciples." The Father is glorified when we bring forth much fruit.

In John 15:16, He says it again: "You did not choose Me, but I chose you and appointed you that you should go and bear fruit, and that your fruit should remain, that whatever you ask the Father in My name He may give you." Are you getting it? God intends us to be fruitful, and He has pledged Himself to ensure that we will have all we need to do so because He has appointed us for this very purpose.

God has made clear from the beginning His divine will for our families. He is a "God of families" as we saw in the first chapter. Jesus was "the lamb for the house" (see Exod. 12:21).

Ultimately, I saw my son wonderfully delivered from drugs and alcohol and he remains free, serving the Lord to this day. My marriage has also gone through much restoration. God gave the victory, but it required my participation.

The Fruit of Her Seed

After Adam and Eve succumbed to Satan's snare, God specifically addressed Eve about the outcome of her action. Part of that address referred to her childbearing. "I will greatly multiply your sorrow and your conception; in pain you shall bring forth children" (Gen. 3:16).

I believe that God was speaking of more here than the physical pain and discomfort women would experience during birth. I believe He was speaking of an ongoing principle.

Now, because of the Fall, children would be born into a fallen world, into enemy territory, there to be lost forever unless something is done. Praise God, something *has* been done! The Redeemer has come. That fact helps no one, though, unless it is received.

I believe God was saying to the woman that her physical labor and travail in childbirth was just the beginning point, that there was an ongoing labor and travail in the Spirit He would ask of her. It would be uncomfortable; it would mean staying "present," emotionally and physically, to the pain and difficulties in the family. It would mean not yielding to the nearly overwhelming temptation to escape through the many strategies of avoidance we have mentioned earlier in the book.

It would require great dedication, patience and faithfulness, but God would be with her. If she would take it on, God would privilege her to help bring forth spiritually through her prayers those whom she has brought forth physically. (Husbands, too, are blessed beneficiaries of this kind of intercession.)

The virtuous woman's effectiveness in prayer is not limited to family, but it begins there. If a woman is married, usually within this framework God will gain her attention to teach her great truths that will make her fruitful far beyond her home.

There is also an added bonus. As the woman gives herself to building her household through warfare and birthing prayers, those she births into the Kingdom of heaven will also be used to put *their* feet on the neck of the enemy. They, too, will enforce calvary's victory!

Give Her the Fruit of Her Hands

The virtuous woman is a warrior woman. She allows God to teach her hands to war and her fingers to fight. She takes her stand against God's enemy, Satan, and refuses to back down until she sees total victory.

She is a woman who will endure a season of pain and discomfort while she intercedes for her household who may not yet have come alive to God, or who are suffering undue attacks of the enemy that threaten to rob or hinder God's plan for them. She travails in the spirit; she cries out to God on their behalf.

She has learned the truth of the parable Jesus taught in Luke 18, that we "always ought to pray and not lose heart" (v. 1). She is like the persistent widow who came continually to the unjust judge saying, "Get justice [avenge me] for me from my adversary" (v. 3). The court case had been settled, she had won the judgment, but her adversary would not yield. Therefore she came continually to the court of the land, as many times as it took, to get legal enforcement of the decision. The unjust judge, finally moved to action by her cries, said, "I will avenge her, lest by her continual coming she weary me" (v. 5).

Jesus declared, "Hear what the unjust judge said. And shall God not avenge His own elect who cry out day and night to Him, though He bears long with them? I tell you that He will avenge them speedily. Nevertheless, when the Son of Man comes, will He really find faith on the earth?" (vv. 6-8).

Jesus is saying, "If an earthly judge will finally be moved to action to fulfill a legal decree, how much more will the Judge of all the earth, the God of the universe, be moved to enforce the decision of the court of heaven, one that He Himself has made! He will do it speedily." Yet

He bears long with us in our ignorance as we learn the truth of all He has accomplished for us. When we are ready to move, He is ready to move on our behalf—speedily! "Nevertheless," He says, "when the Son of Man comes, will He really find faith on the earth?" Will He?

God is looking for a people of faith. Faith that refuses to back down. Faith that knows it has the court of heaven and the Supreme Judge of the universe behind it. Faith that stands in the midst of the battle. Overcoming faith. A dear saint, now with the Lord, defined overcoming faith as "faith that knows it has won while it is still fighting the battle."

In this unprecedented move among women, God is awakening them to their womanhood as He designed and desired it to be from the beginning—women who understand what it means to be a "life-giver" as Eve's name indicates. He is awakening virtuous women, about whom God will declare, "Give her the fruit of her hands, and let her own works praise her in the gates" (Prov. 31:31).

Women, will you be among those whom God so commends? I earnestly pray that you will. I pray that the Holy Spirit will move on these written words and ignite your hearts, and open the eyes of your understanding that you will see and comprehend God's awesome plan to which He has called you.

"Arise!" says the Lord. "Arise from your depression and prostration in which circumstances have kept you. Rise to new life. Shine: Be radiant with hope and purpose. Your light, your understanding, has come. 'The glory of the Lord has risen upon you.' Everywhere you put your foot, God has given it to you. Begin to possess your inheritance, for the 'Commander of the army of the Lord' is with you" (see Isa. 60:1; Josh. 1:2,3; 5:14).

—m—

Something to Think About

- Describe how Satan's enmity against women is played out on earth.
- How are the "eyes of our understanding" opened? To what are they opened?
- Where must our prayers begin?

A God of Purpose

—∼∼—

"I know that You can do everything, and that no

purpose of Yours can be withheld from You."

JOB 42:2

From Genesis to Revelation we see that God is a God of purpose. His plan and purpose were not secret, as we have discovered, but have been publicly declared to the universe from the beginning. Our understanding of His purpose grows, however, as our intimate knowledge of Him grows.

When Job, the writer of the oldest book of the Bible, uttered the words of our opening Scripture verse, he had just walked through a lengthy, confusing and painful trial of his faith. Job had known God before his trial. He was "blameless and upright...one who fears God and shuns evil" (Job 1:8). Now, however, he had come to a deeper understanding of God's ways and character.

Job compares his new understanding with his former knowledge of God and declares, "I have heard of You by the hearing of the ear, but now my eye sees You" (42:5). The "eyes of his understanding" had been opened through a deeper and more intimate knowledge of God that had come to Him by way of great pressure and suffering. Now he not only knew "about" God, but he also knew God Himself. This changed everything!

A New Viewpoint

Job now begins to see things from God's perspective. There has been a vital turning of his center and a personal revelation. He has discovered that life is more about God than it is about him, that it is about how he fits into God's plan, not how God fits into his plan. He also discovered that God's plan is the best plan of all. He has discovered not only that God has a purpose, but also that nothing can hinder that purpose from being fulfilled. "I know that You can do all things," Job now declares, "and that no thought or purpose of Yours can be restrained or thwarted" (v. 2, *Amp.*).

Job's friends also knew "about God." They had uttered many inarguable facts about Him. Yet, God said to them, "you have not spoken of Me what is right" (v. 7). They could talk *about* God and miss God's heart all together. They could be right in their "doctrine" and not really know God at all. Not knowing God's heart, they could know nothing of His real purpose (which is to bring us to a full and accurate knowledge of Himself) and thus they made faulty, poor comforters for Job. As DeVern Fromke declared in *The Ultimate Intention*, if our "center is wrong, everything in our reckoning is wrong."

This change of perspective is the hub of all God wants to do in our lives and is a key element of "purpose."

People of Purpose

"God doesn't set goals for your life and hope they come to pass. God doesn't have a vision for what He'd like your life to become. God only has purpose," writes Bob Sorge in his book *The Fire Of Delayed Answers.*[1]

God is always working out His purpose in our lives. Most of the time, however, like Job, it is only in retrospect, after many months or perhaps years of wondering, that we discover what God's purpose has been all along. Then one day, in absolute elation, we see it. Rather, we see God! We see His heart, we see what He has been after, that He has been working "all things after the counsel of His will" (Eph. 1:11, *NASB*), and we know what His will is. We are changed; we are not the same as we were before, and it is not something we could have done for ourselves. We see that God is a God of purpose, and no one or nothing could hinder that purpose from coming forth! Not our confusion, not our ignorance, not even our seeming inability for a time to cooperate with Him will derail His plan. God is greater than all of it!

This is a principle we can follow through history. Because God has a plan, everything He does fits into the fulfillment of that plan. Each piece, even things that can seem almost inconsequential and ordinary, has a place of significance and purpose. Even in those places, the Lord is directing, leading, guiding to bring us—our families, the Church, even nations of the world—into line with His holy purposes.

Let's journey through Scripture to see how intricately women in particular have been woven into the fabric of God's activity on earth from the beginning. After much study for his book *All The Women in the Bible*, Herbert Lockyer comments, "A continuous sojourn...(for over a year) in the world of Bible women, caused one to realize how intimately they were associated with the unfolding purpose of God."[2]

They were not only beautiful women like Esther, who became a queen, or strong women like Deborah, who served Israel as a judge and prophetess, both of whom were powerfully used by God at critical junctures in Jewish history. God also moved through "ordinary" women, women not in "high office," but in equally powerful, though perhaps less noticeable or "public," ways. He used mothers and sisters—women who just seemed by nature to be doing the most natural thing in the world. Yet, like Job, while in the midst of their circumstances, they were often unaware that they were actually working in concert with God for the furtherance of His plan on earth.

The Divine Destiny of a Nation

To awaken the people, it is the women who must be awakened. Once she is on the move, the family moves and the nation moves (Former Prime Minister Nehru of India).

If you study history you will find that where women have vision that country attained a high position, and where they remained dormant that country slipped back (Indira Gandhi).

Educate a man and you educate one person. Educate a

woman and you educate a nation (*Women of Vision 2000 Newsletter*, November 1992).

Our success as a society and as a nation depends not on what happens in the White House but what happens in your house (Barbara Bush).

So say the people of our day, but this is not new. Think back in Bible history. Have you ever thought about the fact that the divine destiny of a nation, as it related to the purposes of God, lay in the hands of three women? Jochabed, the mother of Moses. Miriam, Moses' sister. And yes, even Pharaoh's daughter, though she was an idolater.

Jochabed was a mighty woman of God, a woman of faith, a "virtuous" woman in the truest sense of the word. She was the mother of three children, all of whom would ultimately become great leaders in Israel: Aaron, who became Israel's first High Priest; Miriam, a gifted musician, who led the praises of Israel; and Moses, one of the nation's greatest leaders of all time. Jochabed obviously invested much in the lives of her children, an example to all of a woman whose "worth is far above rubies" (Prov. 31:10).

Jochabed's influence came at a time of great persecution for the nation of Israel. Because the Jewish people had increased mightily in the land of Egypt, Pharaoh had become afraid of them. There were so many of them and he had been treating them so harshly, he feared that in the event of war they would turn on Egypt and "join our enemies and fight against us" (Exod. 1:10).

As a solution, he determined to diminish the race by infanticide. Pharaoh ordered the Hebrew midwives to kill every male child they helped deliver, thereby hoping to weaken the potential military strength of the nation. "But the midwives feared God, and did not do as the king of Egypt commanded them, but saved the male children alive" (v. 17).

Infuriated, Pharaoh then ordered his own people to join in the slaughter, commanding them, "Every son who is born you shall cast into the river" (v. 22).

During this perilous time, Jochabed's third child was born—Moses, a male baby.

Moses' birth was God's way of setting in motion the deliverance of His people He had been planning for nearly 400 years. They were a people whom He planned to make a great nation through which He would display His glory on earth.

God looked for a woman, a woman of faith, a woman of courage, a woman who would actually be willing to stand in the face of the enemy to have God's will fulfilled on earth. It would be easy to miss the influence of Jochabed's part in all this because she would do it in what would seem a natural, even ordinary, way. She would do it in response to a "mother's heart."

The Fearless Faith of a Woman

When Moses was born, he was a "goodly" or "fair" child, which means "fair to God" (see Heb. 11:23). I wonder what Jochabed was thinking as she looked down at the face of her downy "fair" one. Do you think she sensed the special call of God on his life? Or do you think that as a woman of God she saw all her children as children of destiny, and had determined to raise each one in such a way that they would always be available to God for whatever He purposed in their lives? I think when God looked for a woman, He looked for one who was already doing what He needed her to do, something that looked very ordinary, but would have far-reaching, eternal results.

Hebrews 11:23 also says it was "by faith" Moses was hidden by his parents, "because they saw he was a beautiful [special] child; and they were not afraid of the king's command."

Imagine the day Jochabed placed Moses in that basket among the reeds in the river, knowing the reality of the situation. So many things could go wrong. The current could sweep him away. Surely predatory animals were roaming the area, and no one can count on the weather for long. What if Pharaoh's men found him? What would happen then? Certainly they would follow Pharaoh's decree to cast him to his death in the river. Scripture, however, tells us she was not afraid. Her faith and trust were in God. She merely responded to that quiet, inner leading of God that made no sense to the natural mind, but made perfect sense to a mother's heart, which was also filled with love for God.

Think of the swift intervention of Miriam, Moses' sister, and her courage in moving toward the daughter of Pharaoh, the very one who had issued the decree.

Notice how God moved on the heart of Pharaoh's daughter, an idol-atrous woman, and how He ordered her steps. As she looked at the face of that beautiful baby upon whom the favor and call of God rested, her heart was captivated. She was Pharaoh's daughter, yes—but she was first a woman!

God's purposes would be fulfilled. Nothing could hinder them, not even all the armies of Egypt. This deliverer sent from God would not only be preserved, but he would also be raised right under the nose of Pharaoh, at Pharaoh's expense! God does have a sense of humor.

—⟡—

Because of the faith and trust of Jochabed and Miriam, and even the unwitting response of the heart of Pharaoh's daughter, God was able to use them in an ordinary, yet clear and strategic way.

—⟡—

The response of these three women resulted in God's plan moving one step forward. Because of the faith and trust of Jochabed and Miriam, and even the unwitting response of the heart of Pharaoh's daughter, God was able to use them in an ordinary, yet clear and strategic way.

What about you? Is there one in your household you have always sensed has a call from God on his or her life? Like Jochabed, God will use you to shelter, surround, protect and help bring forth that purpose. He will make even idolaters and idolatrous situations serve to further His plan. Do not lose heart. Stand as a watchman for the members of your family and you "shall rejoice in time to come" (Prov. 31:25).

What Is in You?

Hannah is a woman who, at first glance, might seem barely notewor-thy. Hannah had a fertility problem. The Bible simply says of Hannah that "the Lord had shut up her womb" (1 Sam. 1:5, *KJV*).

Barrenness. What a dreaded state for the women of the East! To be barren was a terrible shame. To live in the same house with your husband's other wife who was able to conceive and bring forth life, as was the case with Hannah, had to be exceedingly painful. The Word says that Hannah grieved and wept bitterly. Neither would she eat. Undoubtedly she was deeply depressed, struggling with hopelessness.

The enemy especially strikes at these times of vulnerability. When we are struggling, trying to make sense out of life, the enemy comes. He sneaks in to lie to us against the character of God, about God's willingness to hear us, His care for us and His desire to help us in the midst of our situation. Satan comes when God has a larger purpose in mind, when He is accomplishing something that will take time, patience and endurance in our lives, at a time when we don't understand. Satan's goal is always to discourage us, to cause us to distrust God and turn us from God's way to our way, just as he did to Eve in the garden. The enemy wanted to use Hannah's situation for her undoing, but God wanted to use it for His own mighty purpose to bring glory to Himself and fulfillment to Hannah's heart.

It is important for us to recognize that God was in the midst of Hannah's barrenness. He was again orchestrating something from heaven for the furtherance of His plan and purpose on earth. We see Him moving according to plan in the "circle of prayer" we mentioned in our previous chapter.

Barrenness was not only Hannah's condition, but it was also the condition of God's people at that time in history. First Samuel 3:1 says "the word of the Lord was rare in those days; there was no widespread revelation." The priesthood was riddled with sin. "Now the sons of Eli [the current High Priest] were corrupt; they did not know the Lord" (2:12).

God longed to share His heart, His Word, with His people. He needed a heart open before Him, an ear that would hear Him, a mouth that would speak for Him.

God looked for someone who would carry the burden in prayer, to actually bring the answer to this problem "to birth" in the spirit first. He found Hannah, a woman yearning over the barrenness of her own womb at the time when He was yearning over the barrenness of the whole nation. He placed the burden in her heart that corresponded to the burden on His own heart. I like the way Arthur Matthews says it in his book

Born for Battle, "The problem was God's, the prayer was Hannah's!"[3]

As Hannah began crying out to God for the satisfaction of what she thought was the yearning of her own heart, she was unaware that she was fulfilling divine destiny. She was doing something that was natural to a woman: she wanted a baby! But so did God.

Yet, in that place of anguish, Hannah was working in cooperation with God, to bring to birth and to bring forth His very plan and purpose for His people. She was, in a sense, the "womb of the Spirit" at that point.

Out of the tears, anguish and travail of this one woman, God was to bring forth one of Israel's greatest prophets. The spiritual destiny of a nation was at stake. God would use the prayers of one woman to make the difference.

Hannah, like Job, experienced a turning of her center. In the beginning she had been crying out for herself. There came a point, however, when her heart was turned to God in a new way, as evidenced by her words: "If you will indeed look on the affliction of Your maidservant and remember me, and not forget Your maidservant, but will give Your maidservant a male child, then I will give him to the Lord all the days of his life" (1 Sam. 1:11).

In essence she was saying, "Now, whatever is mine is Yours: this really is more about You than it is about me." At this point her petition was granted: "And the Lord remembered her" (v. 19). The purpose of God moved another step forward.

What is in you? What is the cry of your heart? Perhaps you find yourself in a state of "barrenness" in an area of your own life, or that of your family—a husband, a child. It looks as though what you have longed to see will not come forth. Let your grief draw you to God, and as you pour your heart out to Him, know that you are working in concert with Him, even as Hannah did, for bringing forth a great man or woman for God. Ask Him to reveal to you His larger purpose for your particular situation. The burdens on your heart are not a mistake; God has placed them there. He wants to incorporate you into the furtherance of His kingdom on earth, for His sake and for your fulfillment.

> Those who sow in tears shall reap in joy. He who continually goes forth weeping, bearing [precious] seed for sow-

ing, shall doubtless come again with rejoicing, bringing his sheaves with him (Ps. 126:5,6).

A Woman of Understanding

Abigail was a woman who had a very difficult marriage. She was married to a man named Nabal, an alcoholic. His name means "fool."

Nabal was a very wealthy man, but one who was cross and ill tempered, surly and snarling—he had a currish disposition. He was "harsh and evil in his doings" (1 Sam. 25:3), a hard and oppressive man who lacked good sense.

At the time of our story, David was in the wilderness of Paran with his troops, where Nabal's shepherds pastured his flocks. Knowing it was sheep-shearing time, a time of feasts with food in abundance for the many hands employed to assist in the shearing, David sent 10 of his young men to make a request of Nabal.

> Greet him in my name....And...say to him...: "Peace be to you, peace to your house, and peace to all that you have! Now I have heard that you have shearers. Your shepherds were with us, and we did not hurt them, nor was there anything missing from them all the while they were in Carmel. Ask your young men, and they will tell you. Therefore let my young men find favor in your eyes, for we come on a feast day. Please give whatever comes to your hand to your servants and to your son David" (vv. 5-8).

David and his men had treated Nabal's shepherds well in the fields and even protected them from marauders. Now he is pleading this kindness to Nabal as ground for the favor he would ask of him. David and his men needed food.

Nabal's response shows the heart, character and disposition of the man. Not only did he deny the request, but he also spoke scornfully of David, the one who was known across the region for his exploits in battle. Of him it was sung in all the cities of Israel, "Saul has slain his thousands, and David his ten thousands" (18:7). Yet Nabal belligerently replies, "Who is David, and who is the son of Jesse? Shall I then take my bread and my water and my meat...and give it to men when I do not know where they are from?" (25:10,11).

David's men returned with the message from Nabal. David's response was immediate. "Every man gird on his sword. Surely in vain I have protected all that this fellow has in the wilderness....he has repaid me evil for good. May God do so, and more also, to the enemies of David, if I leave one male of all who belong to him by morning light" (vv. 13,21,22).

Enter Abigail

One of Nabal's servants ran to apprise Abigail of the situation, knowing they were in serious danger. "But the men were very good to us,...a wall to us both by night and day,...Now therefore, know and consider what you will do, for harm is determined against our master and against all his household. For he is such a scoundrel that one cannot speak to him" (vv. 15-17). Obviously, Nabal was well known by his behavior.

Abigail now has a decision to make. How was she to respond to this grave situation in which she found herself? Undoubtedly, this was not unusual for her; she had lived with this man for some time. This is how he dealt with everyone.

Let's look more closely at Abigail. What kind of a life would she have had with Nabal? She had money, a certain measure of security; her physical needs were met. She had a home, food and clothing. What about her heart, her spirit? Many women know what it is to have wealth and all it provides and still be empty inside.

Abigail's name signifies "joy of her father," which tells me she was the delight of her father's heart. I can imagine she brought pleasure, love and laughter to her father and the household as a young girl. She had a tenderness, a sensitivity, perhaps spontaneity, within her.

Imagine yourself in her situation. She had married and moved away from all she had known. Her marriage would have become a tremendous sorrow to her. It was nothing like any bride would have wanted, let alone dreamed of. Every day she lived with a mean-spirited man. Selfish and self-centered, he cared little for anyone but himself. He was focused on his own needs and no one else's. He was abrupt, lacking in tenderness or sensitivity. He was not a communicator, and cared little about real intimacy.

The first thing Scripture tells us about Abigail is that she was "a woman of good understanding" (1 Sam. 25:3). Only afterward does it mention her beauty.

—*m*—

We need to be reminded of what makes a woman of such immense value to God and then to man. It is not her outward beauty, her appeal, her style, or her hair that makes her desirable; it is her wisdom, her good understanding, her "inner beauty."

—*m*—

In today's world where outward appearance is constantly emphasized as of first and foremost importance, we need to be reminded of what makes a woman of such immense value to God and then to man. It is not her outward beauty, her appeal, her style, or her hair that makes her desirable; it is her wisdom, her good understanding, her "inner beauty."

Abigail had learned some things out of her need, out of her furnace of affliction. In the midst of her own private pain, she had allowed the desire of her heart to be turned from man to God. She had gained an understanding of the will and ways of her God, which alone is wisdom. This was a woman who had come to God with her hurts, pains and disappointments, a woman whose heart had been emotionally broken but spiritually strengthened.

Now the question is put to her, "What will you do in the midst of this grave situation?" As a woman of wisdom, she responded quickly and without fear that she was doing the wrong thing as a woman. Without telling her husband (see vv. 18,19), she prepared the very best of food and sent the servant on before her. As she sited David, "she dismounted quickly from the donkey, fell on her face before David, and bowed down to the ground" (v. 23).

Abigail was not groveling or being manipulative. This was a secure woman, a wise woman. She humbly asks his favor. As she begins to speak, she knows she has something to say, something David needs to hear for his own welfare. It is something that is prophetic regarding God's call on his own life. "Let your maidservant speak in your ears, and hear the words of your maidservant. Please, let not my lord regard this scoundrel Nabal. For as his name is, so is he: Nabal is his name, and folly is with him!" (vv. 24,25).

Abigail is speaking forthrightly, but not in an attitude of vindictiveness, anger or revenge. Her heart has been broken, tenderized, dealt with by God. She has learned His ways. She is merely stating the way things are as evidenced by Nabal's life, his behavior and unwillingness to change. "This is the way of a fool," she is saying to David, "the way of one who refuses to be dealt with by God. He lacks understanding." The spirit of her plea is, "Forgive him for he knows not what he does."

As she continues to speak to David, the anointed future king of Israel, she does so with deference and respect, yet without flattery or manipulative words. Neither does she upbraid him, but endeavors to bring him to a better place in his own reaction to Nabal. "As your soul lives," Abigail declares, "the Lord has held you back from coming to bloodshed and from avenging yourself with your own hand" (v. 26). Because Abigail knows God and His ways, God could use her to express His ways to others—even to a king.

Abigail has learned the restraint of the Lord. She knows that He is a God of purpose. He makes all things right in His own way and time. She knows it is wise to wait on God and not take matters into her own hands. She continues in her address to David:

> "For the Lord will certainly make for my lord an enduring house, because my lord fights the battles of the Lord, and evil is not found in you throughout your days. And it shall come to pass, when the Lord has done for my lord according to all the good that He has spoken concerning you, and has appointed you ruler over Israel, that this will be no grief to you, nor offense of heart to my lord, either that you have shed blood without cause, or that my lord has avenged him-

self. But when the Lord has dealt well with my lord, then remember your maidservant" (vv. 28,30,31).

Abigail was speaking wisdom into David's life. She wanted nothing to mar the glory of God's plan and purpose through him.

David responded with great respect and gratitude.

> "Blessed is the Lord God of Israel, who sent you this day to meet me! And blessed is your advice and blessed are you, because you have kept me this day from coming to bloodshed and from avenging myself with my own hand. For indeed, as the Lord God of Israel lives, who has kept me back from hurting you, unless you had hurried and come to meet me, surely by morning light no males would have been left to Nabal!" So David received from her hand what she had brought him, and said to her, "Go up in peace to your house. See, I have heeded your voice and respected your person" (vv. 32-35).

God sent Abigail to influence David at a critical juncture in his life. David's eternal throne and the ongoing purposes of God on earth were forever affected by her action. Through a woman, the plan of God had taken another step forward.

Through Wisdom a House Is Built

The Spirit-Filled Life Bible comments, concerning this portion of Scripture, "This is one of several instances in Scripture where strong and extremely capable women are used by God in crucial situations. Abigail certainly shows herself worthy to be a queen, standing in stark contrast with Nabal 'the fool.'"[4]

Abigail is a beautiful picture of what God has in His heart for woman. He intended from the beginning that her influence be significant, that she not be silenced or disregarded, but rather respected and received as David did Abigail.

"Through skillful and godly Wisdom is a house (a life, a home, a family) built, and by understanding it is established [on a sound and good foundation]," the *Amplified* version of Proverbs 24:3 tells us. God intended that woman would open her mouth with wisdom—His wisdom—that the house would be built. This is His design for her. Such wisdom, when embraced, brings great honor to one who receives it (see Prov. 4:8,9). It is not impossible to imagine that in this day and hour, as in the case of Abigail and David, the very future of a nation might be affected by a woman's actions.

I think of other women, such as Sarah. She spoke into Abraham's life at a time when God Himself wanted to separate the works of their own hands (Ishmael) from the life of God's Spirit (Isaac) for God's ongoing purpose for their lives and the future of the nation He was forming for Himself (see Gen. 21:8-12).

I think of Esther, mentioned earlier, who risked her life to confront her husband, King Ahasuerus, when all the Jews in the land were about to be annihilated. Such uninvited confrontation was against the law in this heathen kingdom. One was subject to certain death if not received by the king.

Through the instruction of Mordecai (analogous of the Holy Spirit), Esther realized that her life had far greater purpose than merely maintaining her own immediate comfort and status quo. The lives of her people were in great peril, and Mordecai's words, "who knows whether you have come to the kingdom for such a time as this?" pierced her heart. She replied, "I will go to the king,...and if I perish, I perish!" Her center turned and, moving in great wisdom, she became instrumental in the deliverance of God's people from certain ruin (see Esther 4:8-16)

All these women, along with many others in Scripture, were "life givers," both by their actions and by their words.

God has indeed called upon women throughout the centuries to turn and preserve whole nations through their godly wisdom and courage for His own sake and purpose. Yet, for the most part, they have at best remained unrecognized as having specific significance in the plan of God, and downtrodden at worst.

Jesus came to change all that. He came to die for the sin of humanity—the sin that caused separation, hostility, guarded self-protectiveness—for a world in which the weak are vulnerable to the strong. One of the most significant results of His death would be that His Spirit, His life, His power, His authority would be "pour[ed] out...on *all* mankind;...your sons *and* daughters...on the male *and* female...I will pour out My Spirit in those days" (Joel 2:28,29, *NASB*, italics added). In Christ there would be "neither male nor female [no division]...all [would be] one in Christ Jesus" (Gal. 3:28). In Christ there would be a restoration, a coming together of that which Satan had rent asunder.

The Church has been slow to understand. We have been weak at our foundation. The wisdom by which the "house" will be built—individual houses and the House of the Lord—is a corporate wisdom, a godly wisdom that must include male and female, each balancing the other with their own unique contributions. Our strength is in our unity, joined together to express the full image, character and nature of God.

Today we are seeing signs that God is in the process of restoring His original design, that which He purposed from the beginning and fashioned for Himself. Celebrate, Church, take heart! We have God's Word for it: "No purpose of [His] can be withheld from [Him]" (Job 42:2).

—✑—

Something to Think About

- Name the three women upon whom the plan and purpose of God hinged at the time of Moses. Describe the parts they played and how each functioned out of their "natural" womanhood.
- Describe how Hannah's own longing fit into the very purpose of God for that time and how the "circle of prayer" was played out in her life.
- Explain what God wanted to do in Hannah's heart first before He answered her request and how that might apply to some prayers you are praying.

- 12 -

The Hearts of the Fathers

—✺—

"Behold, I will send you Elijah the prophet before the
coming of the great and dreadful day of the Lord.
And he will turn the hearts of the fathers to the
children, and the hearts of the children to their
fathers, lest I come and strike the earth with a curse."

MALACHI 4:5,6

God's prophets were His messengers. As messengers, the prophets throughout history have shared the heart of the unseen God with His people. They declared God's magnificent purposes, His enduring love, His correction, His grief over sin and His longing to have them walk in His ways so they might know His provision, protection and blessing as their Father.

Malachi's name actually means "my messenger." As such, he was used to bring "the final inspired word of scripture until the New Testament."[1]

Dr. James Dobson has been a modern-day messenger to society. He has spoken, and continues to speak, strongly and clearly about the importance of family. In his book *Straight Talk to Men and Their Wives*, Dr. Dobson states,

The western world stands at a great crossroads in its history. Our very survival as a people will depend on the presence or absence of masculine leadership in millions of homes.

Why do I place such importance on the involvement of men in determining the survival of a culture? Because no modern society can exceed the stability of its individual family units, and women seem more aware of that fact than their husbands.[2]

Fatherhood—Center Stage

The subject of fatherhood has never been a peripheral issue with God. It is center-stage stuff! As the Old Testament closes and the final words of inspiration are voiced through Malachi, we hear the heart of the eternal Father as He speaks about the hearts of earthly fathers.

In essence, God is saying through this prophet of old that before the "great and dreadful day of the Lord" (4:5), before the return of Jesus and the final judgment of God, a significant occurrence will take place. The hearts of the fathers and children will be turned to one another, and God will begin with the fathers. This divine turning will be "to make ready a people prepared for the Lord" (Luke 1:17).

Then, to remind us how vital this is to God's plan and purpose, the New Testament opens with a repeat of this word. Just as the Church age is about to begin, as the birth of John, the one who will "Prepare the way of the Lord" (3:4) is announced, we are told what he will do. "He will...go before Him [Jesus] in the spirit and power of Elijah, 'to turn the hearts of the fathers to the children,'...to make ready a people prepared for the Lord" (1:17).

Because this phenomenon is linked in Luke with the coming of John the Baptist, we tend not to associate it with end-time events. The reference in Malachi, though, seems to do so. The *Harper Study Bible* resolves this tension, "This prophecy of the coming of Elijah envisions two fulfillments, one at the First Advent of Christ and the other in connection with the day of the LORD. Christ identified John the Baptist's coming as a preliminary fulfillment of this prophecy."[3]

God wants to do something critical, then, in families before Jesus' return, and it has to do significantly with fathers.

Father Loss

Fatherhood is suffering great fragmentation in today's world. The beginning of the decline is most often linked by historians to the shift of fathers from homes as a result of the Industrial Revolution in the mid-1800s. We have seen it grow, however, to alarming proportions in the past 30 to 40 years.

David Blankenhorn, in his book *Fatherless America*, states,

> Tonight, about forty percent of American children will go to sleep in homes in which their fathers do not live. Before they reach the age of eighteen, more than half of our nation's children are likely to spend at least a significant portion of their childhoods living apart from their father. Never before in this country have so many children been voluntarily abandoned by their fathers. Never before have so many children grown up without knowing what it means to have a father.
>
> Fatherlessness is the most harmful demographic trend of this generation. It is the leading cause of declining child well-being in our society. It is also the engine driving our most urgent social problems, from crime to adolescent pregnancy to child sexual abuse to domestic violence against women. Yet, despite its scale and social consequences, fatherlessness is a problem that is frequently ignored or denied. It remains largely a problem with no name.[4]

The Erosion of Moral and Ethical Ideals

The cost of fatherlessness to us as a society has been so immense that it defies adequate description. No part of our lives has remained unaffected.

William Bennett states in the *Wall Street Journal*, "In seeing the statistical portrait of the moral, social and behavioral conditions of American society, covering a 30 year time span, from the early 1960's until the present...it is shocking to see how precipitously American life has declined...despite enormous governmental effort to improve it."[5]

The percentage of increase in violent crime, illegitimate births, abortion, the divorce rate and teen suicide is shocking, and this from just one Western nation—the United States of America.

Aleksandr Solzhenitsyn put it this way: "The west has been undergoing an erosion and obscuring of high moral and ethical ideals. The spiritual axis of life has grown dim."[6]

Solzhenitsyn identifies the root of the problem. Our cultural decline is merely evidence of our spiritual decline. As America continues to pursue liberal thought, declaring that there are no absolutes, that truth and right are "relative" and subject to each person's interpretation, the spiritual center of our culture has grown dim. Nowhere has this devastating decline been more evident than in the collapse of family values.

The Enemy Comes in Like a Flood

How did we get to where we are today? Has God been caught off guard, or has He been fully aware and fully active in the very center of the destruction? Let's trace the events of the past 40 years and see.

In the mid-1950s, radicals, intellectuals and freethinkers from university campuses across the United States began to give voice to a message that would have devastating effects. The message was simple and short, yet it spoke volumes: "God is dead!" they belligerently pronounced.

In essence, they were saying, "There is no higher power we must answer to. Whatever feels good or seems right to you, do it! There will be no cost, no consequences!"

Scripture and history are replete with evidence that nations rise or fall depending on their moral behavior. America had been built on moral, spiritual principles. These words tore at the very fabric of life as we had known it. The foundation of our nation was under attack and the whole Western world would suffer the fallout.

Thus began a shifting, a turning in the atmosphere that was undeniable. For the Church, it was the beginning of a spiritual warfare that was different from anything it had yet faced.

During this same time frame, surely in answer to many prayers that were being prayed, God began to raise up another voice on earth. The voice was that of Billy Graham, a young, dedicated, articulate evangelist who has preached the gospel to perhaps more people than any other person in history. His message, too, was simple, yet extremely profound: "God loves you, and He has a purpose for your life. Repent, and your sins will be forgiven." God was not dead, but very much alive, and He was fulfilling His promise: "When the enemy comes in like a flood, the Spirit of the Lord will lift up a standard against him" (Isa. 59:19).

With the advent of television in the mid-1950s, the media was now able to enter not only homes, but also the minds of the public. People who would not think of frequenting places where liberal and ungodly viewpoints were being expounded now were unwitting receptacles as the rhetoric found its way into their own living rooms day by day. What originated with seemingly harmless entertainment, such as *I Love Lucy*, as well as programs that had a moral theme, such as *Father Knows Best*, would eventually evolve into a harbinger of values antithetical to God's kingdom. The mind, heart and soul of society would change drastically as the media, journalism and the entertainment industry found new inroads into our increasingly numbed consciences.

By the time the 1960s arrived, we began to see the fruit of the countercultural revolution with its total and utter rebellion against anything of the "establishment." We saw campus riots, free sex, drugs and acid rock. Life as we had known it was rapidly disappearing. What had once been considered appropriate, decent, moral behavior was now being redefined. Our shock at what was happening became less and less noticeable. Our reaction was typical, according to Robert Bork. In his book *Slouching Towards Gomorrah* he writes, "With each new evidence of deterioration, we lament for a moment, and then become accustomed to it."[7] It is the proverbial "frog in the pot" syndrome.

Coming alongside, however, and happening in concert with this moral revolution, was another revolution—a spiritual revolution. The Spiritual Renewal Movement of the late 1960s began, and another "standard" was being lifted.

Radical Secular Feminism

At the dawning of the 1970s, the sexual revolution was in full swing. With it came another expression of dissidence, another voice containing another message escalating in intensity—that of the radical secular feminist camp. Many women were hurting, angry and increasingly dissatisfied with inequities (real and perceived) in our culture. They were mad and they declared that they were not "going to take it anymore!" Some of the issues they raised were legitimate and needed to be addressed. Their agenda was mixed, however, and time and investigation have revealed virulent hidden factors and motives that strike at the very heart and harmony of family life as it has been defined in the past. In fact, no other movement more blatantly attacks traditional family values than that of the radical feminists.

—⁓—

One of the goals of radical feminists is to ensure that women have the means to develop an environment in which they can function completely independent of men.

—⁓—

Robert Bork asserts, "Radical feminism is the most destructive and fanatical movement to come down to us from the sixties. This is a revolutionary, not a reformist, movement....Totalitarian in spirit, it is deeply antagonistic to traditional western culture and proposes the complete restructuring of society, morality, and human nature."[8]

Feminism strikes at the foundation of society. Indeed, it attacks the very heart of God's plan for man and woman and, ultimately, the Church.

Just consider the agenda presented at the Fourth United Nations World Conference On Women held in Beijing, where the platform for action was dominated by feminists from Canada, the United States and Europe. These topics clearly reveal one of the key sources of the splintering of the family, topics such as the redefinition of gender, alternative lifestyles, abortion on demand, sexual freedom for adolescents and children's rights over parental rights. The group's agenda intentionally adds to and exacerbates the breakdown and fragmentation of families that society is so painfully suffering.

One of the goals of radical feminists is to ensure that women have the means to develop an environment in which they can function completely independent of men. We can see this plainly on at least three fronts:

- Economically: Equal pay for equal work was a needed reform, but for many the anger and the real heart motivation behind the demand was the desire to be financially free of the need to depend upon men.
- Sexually: The feminist constituency is heavily comprised of lesbians.
- Reproductively: Artificial insemination serves to perpetuate the illusion that they are a "normal and complete society."

In the midst of all this, there is not only a dismantling of femininity, but also of gender itself, a differentiation that was established by God when He looked at Adam and said, "It is not good that man should be alone; I will make him a helper comparable to him" (Gen. 2:18). Such artificial separating of the sexes to live independently of one another strikes right at the core and heart of God's plan. Its roots are demonic, simply another tactic of the enemy to hinder the purpose of God from being realized on earth. Together, man and woman were to be the image bearers of God. Their destiny was forever wrapped up in their union, in their completion of one another as witnesses of the fullness of God on earth.

The Flight of Fathers

The flight of fathers from the home has come hard on the heels of the feminist agenda. I am not implying that the problem began with the women or that the blame lies only with them. The reasons are multifaceted. I do believe, however, that the reaction of women, in large part, has been because of the failure of men to take their proper place in the family and society. In their disappointment and hurt, many women have hardened their hearts toward men. They have not had a godly perspective of their womanhood and their purpose in God's scheme of things. They have not known how they fit into God's plan. In their woundedness, they have turned away from the men, leaving them in their isolation.

In today's affluent society, women have more options than ever before in history. Many, knowing they can provide for themselves, at least minimally, simply opt out of the marriage altogether. For them, even the added financial stress is a welcome change from the stress of a painful, failing, dysfunctional marriage. Lacking God's perspective, they do not understand how critical the union is, and how necessary both are to the welfare of the children. David Blankenhorn agrees: "Men in general, and fathers in particular, are increasingly viewed as superfluous to family life: either expendable or as part of the problem."[9]

The children, then, are left to suffer the loss, the wreck and ruin of the family caused by the widening chasm between the sexes.

What is the answer to the ever-widening disparity between men and women and the resultant destructive, moral and spiritual problems that are tearing at the fabric of society? Is it social reform? Or is it, as it has ever been, that the Church must become what it was called to be from the beginning—a demonstration to the world of the heart of God? Is this not what God meant when He spoke through the prophet Isaiah, "Darkness shall cover the earth, and deep darkness the people; but the Lord will arise over you, and His glory will be seen upon you. The Gentiles shall come to your light, and kings to the brightness of your rising" (Isa. 60:2,3)?

When Israel was walking with their God, did not the nations around them recognize something distinctly different about them, something that caused them to know "there is a God in Israel" (1 Sam. 17:46)? Was not this always the issue? God was always wanting His people to be a witness to Himself, to His ways, to His beauty and power. His people are to be a witness to His ability to care and provide for them.

"Before Jesus comes to be glorified in the earth, He is coming to be glorified in the church," declares Francis Frangipane.[10] As He comes to fill His Church with His glory, will He not first fill the very substructure of His dwelling place, male and female, with His glory—redeeming, repairing, restoring her to His original intention? Surely He will!

The Father Heart of God

The issue of fatherhood has ever been critical to God's unfolding plan. Our opening Scripture verses taken from Malachi 4:6 indicates that the blessing or cursing of an entire nation rests upon the response of that nation's fathers to their children.

As we have previously mentioned, God is first of all a Father. Everything He is, everything He says, everything He does, flows out of His Father heart. He longs to share Himself, to demonstrate and express His Father heart—His heart of tender mercy and compassion, along with His strength and leadership. He has always wanted the world to see Him, to know Him as He actually is. From the beginning, His plan was that "all shall know Me, from the least of them to the greatest of them" (Heb. 8:11).

Jesus repeatedly said He had come to "show us the Father," that in knowing Him, we would become like Him (see 2 Cor. 3:18). Earthly fathers were to express their heavenly Father to their families. Sadly, this has not always been the case. Could we say, rarely the case?

Many earthly fathers have not been able to love well. Some have been emotionally or physically abusive. Others have been emotionally unavailable to their families, or absent altogether. Consequently, many children and many of us as adults have a faulty view of our Father God. We see Him as disinterested, distant and uncaring. Or perhaps we see Him as a harsh taskmaster, cold, critical, always demanding that we do better. We see Him as one who never really accepts us or loves us in the tender ways that would let us know in the core of our being that we are valued, that we are safe and delightfully welcome in His presence. Thus we become caught in a cycle of hurt, loss, neglect and pain, bringing it with us into our marriages and passing it on to the next generation. The problem is not getting better; it is growing steadily worse.

Is there a way out, a way of recovery? Has God raised up another standard? I believe He has.

The Helper

It is not mere happenstance that at the height of the radical feminist movement, God was raising up a different voice. The feminists' strident voices were being increasingly heard throughout the land crying, "Do your own thing, women! Break free from the shackles! Be liberated from your mundane existence! Devoting yourself to family is a tragic waste of your abilities." God, however, was bringing forth a women's movement of His own. As the Renewal Movement of the late 1960s got under way, one of its most significant effects was that on the hearts of women. During this time, Aglow and many other Christian women's groups came into being, groups that would cultivate and nurture the spiritual growth of the incredible numbers of women flooding into the Kingdom.

The great emphasis of this movement among women was home and family. (Coincidental? I think not!) Women grew and had a new appreciation of God's plan for them, a new understanding of the value God places on life and relationships, a new devotion to see God's plan realized.

This movement was not without pitfalls, however. It started well but got sidetracked into a legalism that, for a time, sabotaged what God had begun. Remember, this was during a time when the whole Western world, men and women alike, were being encouraged to cast off restraint. There was a cry in the land to be free, to be answerable to no one. Perhaps it was in reaction to this flagrant rejection of accountability that dear men of God began to preach a message that waylaid this fresh move of God. These were men whom we loved, from whom we had received much and who, I have no doubt, sincerely desired to see the kingdom of God brought forth.

Extreme, legalistic teaching of submission for women became the word of the day, a word that effectively silenced them in the lives of their husbands and countered the very thing God was beginning to establish. Subsequently the rule-oriented teaching of women evolved into what was called "The Shepherding Movement," which was primarily about men. Men, too, were put under strict authority to other men, creating a "chain of command," which, in essence, taught that one could not be trusted to hear God for himself.

The Renewal Movement floundered, but God was not caught off guard. Time was not wasted as He continued to work—deeply so in the hearts of women—growing them, maturing them spiritually and emotionally. God was preparing the "help" He had designed for the man, waiting for the day when He could present her to him again. That day would depend on the receptivity of the man.

Women have undergone a restoration in these last 30 years. We have achieved a great measure of wholeness. We have learned much about who we are, how we are designed and how purposeful our design is. In today's society, this understanding is more urgent than ever.

Let's revisit the design of woman for a moment because this truth is critical to the welfare of the family, the Church and the nation, and it will help us understand one of the significant ways God will "turn the hearts of the fathers" in this precarious hour.

Marriage by Design

Marriage, although intended to be the source of great blessing and satisfaction, was, from the beginning, also remedial. It was the "remedy" to a problem—the man's aloneness. His condition was "not good." God observed that he would be greatly helped by a wife.

Let's consider for a moment what James Dobson has to say about marriage and the role women play in their husbands' lives. Referring to George Guilder's book *Men and Marriage*, he writes,

> The single male is often a threat to society. His aggressive tendencies are largely unbridled and potentially destructive. By contrast, a woman is naturally more motivated to achieve long-term stability. Her maternal inclinations (they exist in every culture) influence her to desire a home and a steady source of income. She wants security for herself and her children. Suddenly, we see the beauty of the divine plan. When a man falls in love with a woman, dedicating himself to care for her and protect her and support her, he suddenly becomes the mainstay of social order.
>
> Instead of using his energies to pursue his own lusts and desires, he sweats to build a home and save for the future and seek the best job available. His selfish impulses are inhibited. His sexual passions are channeled. He discovers a sense of pride because he is needed by his wife and children. Every one benefits from the relationship. When a society is composed of individual families that are established on this plan, then the nation is strong and stable. It is the great contribution marriage makes to civilization.[11]

All this does not come automatically, however, without plan and purpose, without walking according to the design God intended.

As mentioned, the initial problem God identified, and for which woman was fashioned to resolve, was the "aloneness" of the man. She was designed and equipped in such a way that she would "surround and protect" him against, not only his physical aloneness, but also his emotional aloneness—that part of him that easily remains aloof, isolated and unavailable.

—∾—

The very fact that woman is a relational being first, that she cannot function with integrity for long without conversation, without a sharing of lives, without a connecting on a deeper level than the evening news and still be responsive and passionate in the bedroom, is all part of God's design.

—∾—

Woman was designed physically, emotionally and sexually to help man. The very fact that woman is a relational being first, that she cannot function with integrity for long without conversation, without a sharing of lives, without a connecting on a deeper level than the evening news and still be responsive and passionate in the bedroom, is all part of God's design. Because her sexuality is deep within her, in order to access his wife's body in an ongoing, increasingly meaningful way, a man must learn to come out of himself emotionally and access her heart. To have a truly fulfilling relationship with her, a man must be drawn into a deeper place, beyond the physical passions of his body to his own heart that he might share it with her.

Though he may find this uncomfortable at first, and may not fully comprehend what his wife is needing from him, it is essential that he understand this is not just a selfish demand on her part, nor is it a "woman thing." It is, in fact, a "God thing." God has placed in the heart of woman the deep need for emotional intimacy, and He did it purposefully. The health of the family depends on it.

Marriage is the primary arena God has provided in which to repair the old hurts, to restore the damage that isolates, that drives each of us inside ourselves and makes us hostile to others (if only secretly), but particularly so for the man. Here, in relationship with his wife in whom his heart can "safely trust" (see Prov. 31:11), God intended to begin to bring the man to wholeness.

As the husband is beckoned out of his aloneness, his heart becomes enlarged to truly know his wife, to live with her according to understanding. With this communion comes a greater knowing on at least four additional levels.

First, not only does he come to know his wife more intimately, but he also comes into a deeper knowledge of his own heart. As he becomes "present" to her, he becomes present to himself. In that "mirrored" relationship, not only her heart, but also his own heart, is reflected as well. John Powell, who writes much about relationships and personal wholeness, declares that we can know only as much of ourselves as we have had the courage to confide in others.[12]

Paul Tournier concurs when he says, "He who would see himself clearly must open up to a confidant freely chosen and worthy of such trust."[13] How beautifully the dynamics of marriage, as God intended them to operate, provide for the kind of safety where such personal growth can take place!

Second, the man's relationship with the Lord is affected. Our relationship with others, 1 John 4:7,8 tells us, reveals the genuineness of our relationship with God. This has ever been God's design, and surely one of His main reasons for not wanting the man to remain alone. Often the failure of relationship with those closest to us convicts us of our true condition before God. One can be "born again" and yet remain emotionally closed to God and to others, and thus remain emotionally and spiritually immature.

The third level of "knowing" relates to our Scripture verses at the beginning of this chapter. As the hearts of men are enlarged to receive and know their wives, often through this union their hearts are prepared and opened to emotionally encompass their children as well.

When a man begins to feel that it is "safe" to be emotionally vulnerable, he becomes able to provide that emotional safety to those around him. The children become beneficiaries of their father's newfound freedom. Marilyn Williamson, wife of my former pastor, often says, "What leaves the heart, reaches the heart." Children begin to sense the safety in their father's heart and his emotional presence in their lives. As a result, they begin to respond in kind. Automatically, though it may take awhile if the damage has been great, their hearts will become "turned to their fathers."

Rick Joyner, founder and executive director of Morningstar Publications, recently commented, "There are no fathers without a woman present....There are many teachers, but few fathers. God is longing to see fathers come forth." A man's relationship with his wife is critical to this process.

This home arena is the springboard for nearly everything else of value a man will do in life. Here he learns the skills necessary to society as a whole.

To a man who has become known in his own home, a fourth level of "knowing" opens up. As the husband of a virtuous woman in whom his heart has learned to safely trust, he will become "known in the gates, when he sits among the elders of the land" (Prov. 31:23). The church and community will reap the overflow of the restored intimacy in relationship between the husband and wife. Those who would lead and manage the church, we are told in 1 Timothy 3:4,5, must have learned how to gently lead and manage their own homes first. A true shepherd's heart requires the same skills, the same vulnerability and presence in relationship, the same kind of commitment and love, only on a larger scale.[14]

It is interesting that, although Adam was eventually to have dominion over the earth, he was first instructed to "keep" (guard and protect) the garden, his home, the place where he lived. Because he did not do so, the enemy entered. Adam lost not only the garden, but the earth as well. This is a lesson for us today.

Eve, through ignorance, failed to be the help the man needed. As a result of their combined actions, a civil war began at the core of God's crowning creation—male and female—which carries on to this day. The world continues in great chaos, destruction and confusion.

Deep darkness truly has covered the earth, but our light, the Church's light, has come. We are seeing God's original intention. We know the answer. Our strength will come only in the reconciling of male and female at a level never before known by us. When the homes are in order, when the hearts of men and women are appropriately engaged in appreciation of one another as God designed them to be, the automatic outflow will be that the Church will be in order.

Let us seek the Lord for wisdom; let us humble ourselves before Him and ask Him to reveal attitudes in our hearts that may be hindering His purposes from coming forth in this day and hour.

Above all, let us remember that no purpose of God's will be withheld from Him, and take comfort from the words of God's messenger, Malachi. It is a prophetic word of promise:

> But to you who fear My name the Sun of Righteousness shall arise with healing in His wings (4:2).

—⚏—

Something to Think About

- What are some events in our recent history (the last 40 years) that have contributed to the present condition of the Western world?
- Describe how the ideology of women in the secular world has been affected by these events. What are some corresponding events during the same time frame that let us know God has not been caught unaware?
- Describe what God has been doing in the hearts of Christian women in the last 30 years and His purpose in it.

- 13 -

I Will Not Go Without You

—∞—

And Barak said to her, "If you will go with
me, then I will go; but if you will not go
with me, I will not go!"

JUDGES 4:8

Israel was once again doing evil in the sight of the Lord, and once again
the Lord sold the people into the hand of their enemies. This time it
was King Jabin of Canaan who for 20 years "harshly oppressed the children of Israel" until in their desperation they cried out to the Lord for
help. And God sent help—by way of a woman. Her name was Deborah.

Deborah was a prophetess, which speaks of her relationship with
God. She was also noted as the wife of Lapidoth, which indicates she
had a proper relationship with her husband. She was also a judge, or
leader, in Israel. Only two people are mentioned in Scripture as being
both judge and prophet. Samuel was one, Deborah the other.

"Judges were...judicial arbiters, they were (also) 'deliverers,' charis-
matically empowered by God's Holy Spirit for the deliverance and
preservation of Israel."[1]

Though Deborah had a prominent position in society and also had
the call of God on her life, she was comfortable in her role as wife and
homemaker. Scripture does not indicate that she chafed under this
role, even though she was obviously a very gifted stateswoman.

Whether Deborah had children is not mentioned. If she did, they may have reached a certain maturity by this time in her life.

Deborah had the love and encouragement of her husband. In that day and age it is unlikely she could have become the leader she did without his support. He was secure enough and humble enough to recognize God's call on her life and allow her to be used in an incredible, powerful way. Such freedom did not diminish his identity at all—she was, after all, spoken of as "Lapodith's wife." Because he is mentioned by name, he, too, was likely a man of some renown.

Deborah was the political and judicial head of the nation and was greatly respected by those who served her, as well as by all Israel. Her exemplary leadership abilities did not spring from natural talent; rather, they were the result of her close relationship with God.

As a prophetess, she was able to hear the Word and the heart of the Lord and then declare it to others. Her name literally means "bee," from the "sense of orderly motion" and "systematic instincts."[2] The Hebrew root of her name is *dabar*, which denotes "to arrange; but used figuratively [of words] to speak."[3] According to the *Gesenius Hebrew and Chaldee Lexicon* it means "to put words in order."[4]

From all we have learned about woman's design, the way God made her to function, we should not be surprised that this woman's leadership was specifically linked, even by her name, to her ability to "speak," to hear and to communicate the Word of the Lord with clarity and understanding.

Because of her intimate relationship with God, she was also a warrior, a military leader who moved with great wisdom and authority. Once Deborah was assured she had heard from God, she moved quickly to put His mandate into action.

In this case, she had heard by the Spirit that it was time to end the oppression of King Jabin. She summoned Barak, commander of the armies of Israel, a man who is listed among the great men of faith in Hebrews 11:32.

"Has not the Lord God of Israel commanded, 'Go and deploy troops...and I will deliver [the commander of Jabin's army] into your hand'?" Deborah asks (Judg. 4:6,7). Barak's response is interesting. Though he is a military man, a man of great strength, experienced in military conflicts, this time something is different. His reply gives witness to his great admiration and confidence in this woman: "If you will go with me, then I will go; but if you will not go with me, I will not go!" (v. 8).

Even though he is told he will not get full honor for the victory (in this particular battle a woman named Jael will deliver the death blow to the enemy's head—see vv. 9,21) he does not care.[5] "If you will go with me...to direct me and advise me, and in every difficult case to let me know God's mind, then I will go...Barak values the good success of his enterprise more than his honour and therefore will by no means drop his request," Matthew Henry comments.[6]

The issue for Barak and for the armies of Israel was not whether a woman was present, but the successful outcome of the war. He cared more for the welfare of the nation than for his individual reputation. He also knew that their combined efforts, each bringing their particular strengths, would ensure the victory. And victors they were.

> So on that day [the day Barak and Deborah joined forces and went to war against their enemies] God subdued Jabin king of Canaan in the presence of the children of Israel. And the hand of the children of Israel grew stronger and stronger against Jabin king of Canaan, until they had destroyed Jabin king of Canaan (vv. 23,24).

What a celebration followed!

> Then Deborah and Barak...sang on that day, saying: "When leaders lead in Israel, when the people willingly offer themselves, bless the Lord!" (5:1,2).

The leaders had led and the Lord was blessed. The issue was not male or female; the issue was the anointing, the call and equipping of God that made them leaders, male *and* female.

On Sons and Daughters

Just as the coming of the spirit of Elijah to turn the hearts of the fathers (mentioned in our previous chapter) has a twofold fulfillment, so the message in Joel 2:28,29 referring to the outpouring of God's Spirit indicates a similar pattern. Some refer to it as "the former and latter rain" of God's Spirit (see v. 23)—the former at Pentecost after Christ's resurrection and the latter an increasing measure of His Spirit poured out just before He enters into the judgment of the nations mentioned in Joel 3.

What made this promise especially significant was that God's Spirit would be poured out on *everyone* who would repent and call upon the name of the Lord. No longer would there be an elect few. Every class of people—young, old, slave, free, rich, poor, Jew, Gentile (of every race), male and female—would be included in this infilling and equipping by God's Spirit to be changed into His likeness and represent Him to the world. It would be the ultimate reconciliation of Christ's Body for the purpose of the ultimate showing forth of His glory on earth.

—∞—

The most radical part of [God's] promise...
was that His Spirit would be poured out on females.
There would be a reconciliation between every
race, every cultural class.

—∞—

"That they all may be one,....Father,....that the world may believe that You sent Me" (John 17:21), prayed Jesus for His Body. In essence Jesus was saying, "It will take all of them, in love and in union with one another, to truly display all that I am."

The most radical part of the promise, however, was that His Spirit would be poured out on *females*. There would be a reconciliation between every race, every cultural class—but male and female? The Jewish culture could hardly imagine such a thing! At that time, women could not even be formally educated in Jewish religion. Now Joel was announcing they would have the full anointing of God! Not only would the "daughters" receive this inaugural blessing, but also *female slaves* (handmaidens), those who had the fewest rights, the lowest class within the classes!

Their response may be more like ours in our day than we would like to admit. Although we have gladly received Joel's announcement and have made great strides in mending the breach between denominations and races, we have yet to experience in full measure the reconciliation of the most critical part of Christ's Body. To a great extent, the divide still exists between that part of which it was first announced would be the image and likeness of God, that part which first suffered the terrible fissure, that part which is the foundation of each race and each denomination—male and female.

God, however, *is* moving us forward into a new day. He is revealing His heart for His people. He is moving to reconcile us, not only as a corporate Church and as couples, but also as individuals. He is reconciling us to ourselves at the core of our being. Before women could fully move into their designed place, much healing had to occur. Years of demoralizing hurt, discrimination and disrespect needed to be healed. The one person in Scripture who I think vividly exemplifies the condition of women down through the centuries is the bent-over woman of Luke 13.

A Woman Set Free from Bondage

Some of the most moving incidents recorded in biblical history are often of faceless, nameless people, and frequently they are women. It is as though it was not their names that were important, but the vast numbers they represented who would personally identify with them. Down through history, they would continue to speak as millions would be touched and ministered to by their stories.

Such is the case with the woman in Luke 13 who had lived with a spirit of infirmity for 18 long years. *The Living Bible* says she was "seriously handicapped" (v. 11).

Strong's Concordance tells us infirmity (*astheneia*) means "feebleness, frailty, weakness, without strength."[7] This infirmity caused her to be bent over double (see v. 11). She was unable to look up. If you had met her, she would not be able to look at you or meet your eye. Her eyes were always cast down; her only view was of the ground.

This is a picture of many women—handicapped, unable to straighten themselves. In my ministry, I have had the privilege of traveling to about 70 nations of the world. Much of my time is spent talking and sharing with women, listening to what they have to say, encouraging them with the Word of the Lord. No matter what their culture or individual circumstances, I find many bowed low with the hurts of life, the concerns of marriages and families. Many struggle with a deep inner sense of woundedness and inferiority about themselves as individuals, but specifically as women. Their low self-worth and little sense of value can readily be seen on many of their faces. They are clear evidence of the enemy's strategy to weaken and render women powerless and useless, in their own eyes as well as others. Marriages, the home and the church have been weakened everywhere by Satan's insidious tactics.

Scripture says simply of the infirm woman in Luke 13 that she "could in no way raise herself up" (v. 11). She was utterly unable to straighten herself, neither could she function in a normal way as God would have intended. She was held in bondage and was helpless to do anything about it. Jesus said she was a woman "whom Satan has bound" for 18 long years (see v. 16).

It is interesting to note where Jesus found this woman. She was in the "church"! Although she was infirm and her movement was greatly restricted, she wanted to be in the synagogue among the Lord's people on the Sabbath. She obviously loved God.

As Jesus was teaching, He looked out over the crowd and His attention turned toward this woman. Taking the initiative, He called out to her: "Woman!"

Imagine the thoughts that must have raced through her mind at that moment! Embarrassment? Wonderment? *Why is He calling out to me in the middle of the Sabbath service?* Hope? Expectancy? Had she heard of His great powers?

The cumbersomeness of her movement would have made it difficult for her to get anywhere quickly, let alone to the One teaching that morning. But He had called to her. He had taken note of her, even above all others seated there.

As she moved toward Him, she began to hear words of life and healing. Her ears, her mind, could hardly take it all in. "Woman, you are loosed from your infirmity" declared Jesus (v. 12). Even before she called, He had answered. She had not sought Him for His favor, but He had taken the initiative. Though she could in no way raise herself up, Jesus, the Great Physician, now standing before her, was raising her with words of compassion and life. "Woman," Jesus told her, "you are free from your condition, from your inability to function as intended, from your frailty and weakness, from your suffering and pain. Be healed!"

When He laid His hands on her, she was immediately made straight. In a moment of time, what had once been crooked was made straight. She stood erect, healed from her crippled condition, delivered from the shame brought about by her sense of defectiveness. She was able now to look into people's eyes, to talk with them face-to-face, and to function as God had originally designed.

The Indignant Response

The ruler of the synagogue was indignant over the actions of Jesus. He demanded to know why Jesus had healed this woman on the Sabbath. Jesus, as He so often did, answered the question with a question of his own. "Ought not this woman, being a daughter of Abraham, whom Satan has bound...for eighteen years, be loosed from this bond on the Sabbath?" (v. 16).

Jesus identified her as a "daughter of Abraham." "He was using this term in its full spiritual significance," declares G. Campbell Morgan, "as revealing her faith in God."[8] Matthew Henry goes on to say, "She is therefore entitled to the Messiah's blessings"[9] (the blessing of wholeness, restoration, victory over her enemies, an inheritance of mandate and purpose). She is a daughter of the covenant.

A New Question

In these past 25 to 30 years, as I have observed the unprecedented moving of God's Spirit in women around the world in such unusual ways and in continually increasing numbers, as I ponder the meaning of all He has been doing, I believe the Spirit of God has been sent forth in the earth to again ask Jesus' question:

> Ought not this woman, being a daughter of Abraham [a believer in the Messiah, a daughter of the covenant and recipient of the promises], ought not she be set free from all the bondages of Satan?

Has not Jesus, in fact, come to set free all who believe in Him as Messiah from the bondages of the Fall—the devastation Satan, God's enemy, brought about in the garden? Has not the Son of God been sent to bring again the kingdom of God as He purposed and desired it from the beginning? The enemy of God fears one thing more than all others— that the Body of Christ would finally awaken to its true identity and begin to function as the heirs of Christ that we in fact are—together!

The Heart of the Issue

Such is the purpose behind this deep work of healing God has been doing in the heart of woman. Incapable of raising herself, God, by His Spirit, has been awakening and reconciling her to her womanhood as He meant it to be. She is being awakened to her birthright and inheritance, not only for herself, but also as an initial step toward the fullness of all God has ordained for her.

It is imperative that this reconciliation occur within her own heart and spirit first. As all the "crooked places" of shame, hurt and anger are healed, she is then free to be the "help" to her husband, her family and ultimately the cities and nations of the world.

The restoration God desires for women is not about positions on church boards; it is not about whether they can be pastors or leaders and still be "doctrinally correct." We can (and do) have women in all these positions. Today, as in the early New Testament Church, we have women such as Junia, who was named among the apostles in Romans 16:7.[10] We have women such as Phoebe, a deacon (or deaconess), specifically identified as a leader or manager of the things of God who, at times, worked with Paul (see Rom. 16:1,2).[11] There are women such as Priscilla, a teacher of both men and women (see Acts 18:24-26).

Yet we are still missing God's heart. Although we have women functioning in all these roles, we are still nervous about it, uncomfortable, unsure that it is fully appropriate. The reason is that the issue goes much deeper than that. It is not about whether women can teach or hold offices in the Church. It is about the image of God, the likeness and glory of God being manifested in the Church, male and female. It is about both coming together as He designed it from the beginning. It is about respect that comes from a *heart revelation* of the vital contribution of both male and female, and the devastation that results when either is missing or not functioning.

Together, we will be fully equipped to expose the works of darkness and counter the lies the enemy has perpetrated throughout the ages.

—⟋⟍—

Often in history, when the nation of Israel was in trouble, God called for the women.

—⟋⟍—

Together, we will devastate the enemy's camp and take back what he has stolen from us—and from God! When we truly understand that, our struggle will end.

Call for the Mourning Women

Often in history, when the nation of Israel was in trouble, God called for the women. When death was creeping into the cities and nations, into the streets and homes, He called for the women who knew how to pray, to make a difference in the situation. Such is the case in Jeremiah 9. God had sent the people a mourning prophet, but the prophet was not being heard. Now God calls for the mourning women. This is a portion of Scripture that could be accurately applied to conditions in our day:

> Thus says the Lord of hosts, "Consider and call for the mourning women, that they may come; and send for the wailing women, that they may come! And let them make haste, and take up a wailing for us, that our eyes may shed tears, and our eyelids flow with water. For a voice of wailing is heard from Zion, 'How we are ruined! We are put to great shame, for we have left the land, because they have cast down our dwellings.'" Now hear the word of the Lord, O you women, and let your ear receive the word of His mouth;

teach your daughters wailing, and everyone her neighbor a
dirge. For death has come up through our windows; it has
entered our palaces to cut off the children from the streets,
the young men from the town squares (vv. 17-21, *NASB*).

I believe God has again been calling for the mourning, praying
women. This unprecedented move of God in the last 30 years has raised
up a great army of interceding, warring women. He has awakened us,
fashioned us, opened our eyes to understand His purposes on earth. As
we have looked about us with new eyes, our hearts have been greatly
grieved. Truly the earth has become a dark place. Drug addiction, rapes,
shootings of children and young men used to be far removed from the
average person. Today, none of us escape the daily report on the evening
news of these violent events not many miles from our own homes,
sometimes right in our own neighborhoods. Our "children are being cut
off from the streets and our young men from the town squares!"

For many women, the great substance of their prayers has been for
their husbands, the fathers of their children. Today we are seeing vast
evidence that God has begun to move and answer those prayers in a
mighty way.

An Unprecedented Move Among Men

Verse 19 in our Jeremiah 9 portion of Scripture declares, "For a voice
of wailing is heard from Zion, 'How we are ruined! We are put to great
shame.'" The *Bethany Parallel Commentary* says, "Some make this to
be the song of the mourning women. *It is rather an echo to it,
returned from those whose affections were moved by their wailings*"
(italics added).[12] Those for whom the women were wailing were now
responding. Their understanding was being opened and they were seeing their true condition.

In our day, a yearning has been stirring in the heavens, in the very
heart of God Himself, that has been picked up on earth by His handmaidens. We have prayed and we are beginning to hear a response
coming out of Zion.

Randy Phillips, president of Promise Keepers, recently appeared on
national television, and spoke with much feeling when he said,

For years and years the Lord's daughters—our mothers, our wives—have cried out to God. These women have seen the misuse of masculine strength, they've seen men who name the name of Jesus abandon their homes. They've seen men victimize them, tragically, physically, emotionally and sexually.

They see men not standing up and being active in the church. They see communities in decay and they've been crying out to God....Those tears were seeds that were planted in the ground and by the mercy of God He is giving hope because He is resurrecting a right heart in His sons. We are beginning to see our sin and turn to him.[13]

Even as we have spoken in this book about the unprecedented move among women, God has begun another unprecedented move, this time among men. In the past five years, we have seen a corporate move among men such as never before in history. Stadiums across America are filled to overflowing with men who have come together to worship God, to acknowledge their sin of neglect and passivity. Men are pledging to become the husbands, fathers and godly influences in their communities that God so desires.

Some have described it as a grassroots movement God has raised up through which He will deliver a message to this nation—that we need to come back under the sovereign hand of God in this country.

One of the great emphases of this movement is fatherhood. Men are awakening to the fact that one of the most critical tasks of a man's life is to be an involved, responsible father to his children. "It's as if our male culture were collectively looking at their watches and saying, 'It is five o'clock, time to go home.'"[14] God is beginning to "turn the hearts of the fathers to their children."

Why Such a Move Among Men?

Dave McCoombs, national director for Man to Man Ministry (Campus Crusade), when asked by Josh McDowell why he thought there was such a move among men at this time, answered that he believes it is because there is a real crisis in masculinity, particularly in the United

States. Men have become confused about their identity, function and sense of value. "It is coming out of the desperation of men's hearts," he explained. "The things they have held up for themselves in terms of identity are collapsing around them."[15]

The crisis in masculinity occurred because of the crisis in femininity. We initially caught wind of it when angry, militant women rose up in the 1960s and 1970s, demanding to be heard.

Many things were not right between the sexes; there were many inequities and abuses, but the answer of the feminists was to declare war, to make it a power struggle, to pit the sides against one another. The "status quo" between male and female was forever overturned.

Men had no idea how to respond, and understandably so. The feminist answer was one of competition, not completion, one where there was no real room for men. Women (of the feminist mind-set) would now strive to be in control, to call the shots, believing that until now this had been the prerogative of men.

How typical of the enemy's tactics! When God is about to do something, Satan will attempt to pervert, abort and destroy, even as he did in the Garden of Eden. He knew that God, before Jesus comes again, will "restore all things [spoken of by the prophets]" (Matt. 17:11). Because he had been there at the beginning and heard God's mandate to Adam and Eve, he also knew that the union of the man and woman would be a critical restoration of the last days. One of the ways he could be sure to prevent it would be to bring even greater disrepute to women. If he could stir them up to be loud, boisterous, militant and hostile, that union would become more and more impossible.

God, however, is never caught short. He allows Satan to function only as far as it serves His purpose. We needed correction as a society, and as the Church. What Satan meant for evil, God has meant for good (see Gen. 50:20). We needed to reevaluate what God wanted of us, particularly as male and female, and he would use the pain of our failing circumstances to get our attention.

Don't Miss What God Is Doing

"Women sense that man has lost touch with what he was truly created to be. He has traded his masculine heritage for a false sense of manhood and God is removing the false props so men are desperately reaching out for authentic manhood," explained McCoombs, in the previously mentioned interview with Josh McDowell, adding, "God is answering the prayers women have prayed over the years."

Later he went on to say, "Men need the respect of women more than anything. Men lost the respect of woman in the garden and we've been fearful and fought this sense of inadequacy for generations and generations."

God is calling us as women to be alert to what He is doing today, to be open to receive our men, to receive what God is doing in their lives. God also wants to reconcile men at the core of their being, to their identity, specifically as men as God designed them to be. We need to recognize that they need our help and our support, not our anger. We must let go of the hurts of the past. Both of us, male and female, have been living lives bolstered with "false props," to use Dave McCoombs's term. False props is just another way of saying we have been wearing masks, building false identities and depending on our flesh to make ourselves acceptable and worthwhile in this world, in the church and in our marriages. The cost of such false self-projection has been staggering! We have been caught in a false, worldly system and have reaped the whirlwind with them, even though we have sincerely and intently determined to follow the Lord.

Dean Sherman, of the College of Christian Ministries at Youth With a Mission (YWAM), University of the Nations, says in one his sermons, "Living by the world system is not just doing worldly things...It is a false basis of identifying yourself." It is a false basis of determining our identity and sense of value. It is looking outside the plan and ways of God to a world in which the enemy has wreaked havoc.

God desires to set us free today, free of ourselves, free from the image building and self-protection that keeps us self-focused and impotent in the plan of God.

Where the Lord Commands the Blessing

The bottom line of everything Jesus came to do was to restore relationship—with God and with each other. He came to destroy the "works of the devil." The works of the devil, then and now, are alienated, fragmented relationships. Sin, at its core, is the failure to love others. All the problems in the world—from wars between nations, the fracturing of our culture, divisions in the Church or divorce between couples—are problems of relationship.

When our relationships are right, when we are walking in true intimacy with God and others, we will have a testimony before the world that those who are truly seeking the meaning of life will be unable to resist. It is this, our genuine love for one another, that Jesus said would testify of His life in us (see John 13:34,35). His disciples would not be recognized by physical healings, nor by miracles, signs or wonders, as wonderful and exciting as these are, but by love. In the atmosphere of such love, God's anointing for the miraculous and the power that "breaks the yoke" of our enemies is poured out.

> Behold, how good and how pleasant it is for brethren to dwell together in unity! It is like the precious oil upon the head, running down on the beard, the beard of Aaron, running down on the edge of his garments. It is like the dew of Hermon, descending upon the mountains of Zion; for there the Lord commanded the blessing—life forevermore (Ps. 133).

The oil represents the anointing of the Holy Spirit. In unity there is anointing and life. In unity God commands the blessing! Until that unity comes to the very core of God's creation—male and female—it will not have reached its complete fulfillment. It is no accident of nature that it takes both male and female to bring forth life. This was God's design. The absence of either produces emptiness, barrenness and impotence. The world will not fully see Jesus until the foundation of His house is fully repaired.

What will be our response as a Church in this day and hour, at this most turbulent time in our history when God is calling us to increased presence and spiritual effectiveness in this dying world? Let us consider the question and then respond to each other, male and female, as Barak did: "I will not go without you!" Indeed, God would say, "You *cannot* go without each other. The life, the power, the victory will come from your union! It is there I gave my blessing. From the beginning I have said, 'Let them, male and female, rule and have dominion over the earth.' I have not changed my plan. As I have said, so shall it be!"

> O, Lord! Let there be a great restoration such as has never been seen in the earth before, male and female, the foundation of Your House, joined together in respect, in honor, valuing one another as indispensable to Your plan. Let us go forth in might, in power, in the full revelation of Jesus Christ on earth according to Your original design, fulfilling our mandate declared at the beginning of time. For Your sake, Lord, for Your glory, for Your purpose, we pray! Amen and amen. So be it!

Something to Think About

(You may want to read the record of Deborah in Judges 4—5 before considering these questions.)

- List the several roles Deborah filled in her life and how you think she functioned in them.
- Describe Barak's attitude toward her and why you think he had such confidence in her.
- What constituted both Deborah and Barak as leaders? Describe what happened when the "leaders" led.

Notes

—⁂—

All references to Webster's are taken from *Webster's New World Dictionary of the American Language*, ed. David B. Cruralnik (New York: The World Publishing Co., 1962).

Introduction

1. Rick Joyner, *MorningStar Prophetic Bulletin* (May 1996).
2. Frances Frangipane, *The House of the Lord* (Lake Mary, Fla.: Creation House, 1991), p. 27.

Chapter 1

1. DeVern Fromke, *The Ultimate Intention* (Cloverdale, Ind.: Sure Foundation, 1963), p. 29.
2. *Theological Wordbook of the Old Testament* (hereafter *TWOT*) ed. by R. Laird Harris, Gleason L. Archer Jr., and Bruce K. Waltke (Chicago: Moody Press, 1980), #437.
3. A. W. Tozer, *Best of Tozer* (Grand Rapids: Baker Book House, 1978), p. 162.
4. The Greek verb *onomadzo*, to give or call a name, comes from the noun *onoma*, which carries with it the full authority, character and reputation of the person named. See *Theological Dictionary of the New Testament* (hereafter *TDNT*) ed. by Gerhard Kittel (Grand Rapids: Wm. B. Eerdmans Publishing Company, 1967), Vol. V, p. 242ff. Also see *A Greek-English Lexicon of the New Testament and Other Early Christian Literature* (hereafter *BAGD*), ed. by Walter Bauer, William F. Arndt, F. Wilbur Gingrich and Frederick Danker (Chicago: The University of Chicago Press, 1957; revised edition, 1979), p. 570ff. Also see *The New Strong's Exhaustive Concordance of the Bible* (hereafter *Strong's*) (Nashville: Thomas Nelson Publishers, 1984), #3686 and #3687.
5. David Blankenhorn, *Fatherless America* (New York: HarperCollins, 1996), p. 1 (Introduction).

Chapter 2

1. *TDNT* 3:520; *BAGD* 409a. See also *Strong's* #2602.
2. Fromke, *The Ultimate Intention*, p. 32.
3. *TDNT* 7:965, 1132; *BAGD* 801b. See also *Strong's* #4991, root: #4982.
4. Wayne Grudem, *Systematic Theology: An Introduction to Biblical Doctrine* (Grand Rapids: Zondervan, 1994), p. 442. See also *Strong's* #6754.
5. *TWOT* #2103, #2104. Also *The Brown-Driver-Briggs Hebrew and English Lexicon* (hereafter *BDB*) (Peabody, Mass.: Hendrickson Publishers, 1996; reprinted from the 1906 edition), p. 915ff. See also *Strong's* #7235.
6. *TWOT* #951; *BDB* p. 461b. See also *Strong's* #3533.
7. For other instances where subdue (*kabash*) is used, see Josh. 18:1; 2 Sam. 8:11.
8. *TWOT*, #951.
9. *TWOT* #2121, #2111; *BDB* p. 921-922. See also *Strong's* #7287.
10. Jack Hayford, General Editor, *Spirit-Filled Life Bible* (Nashville: Thomas Nelson Publishers, 1991), p. 1195.
11. Donald Grey Barnhouse, *The Invisible War* (Grand Rapids: Zondervan Publishing House, 1965), p. 51.

Chapter 3

1. *TWOT* #1553; *BDB* p. 713a. See also *Strong's* #5647.
2. *TWOT* #2104; *BDB* p. 1036b. See also *Strong's* #8104.
3. Watchman Nee, *Messenger of the Cross* (New York: Christian Fellowship Publishers, 1980), pp. 136-137.
4. Fromke, *The Ultimate Intention*, pp. 60-61.
5. *TWOT* #85; *BDB* p. 37b. See also *Strong's* #398.
6. *The New Englishman's Hebrew Concordance*, J. P. Green, ed. (Peabody, Mass.: Hendrickson Publishers, 1984), #398.
7. W. E. Vine, *An Expository Dictionary of New Testament Words* (Grand Rapids: Fleming H. Revell Co., 1966), p. 319.
8. Nee, *Messenger*, pp. 130-131.
9. Ibid., p. 109,
10. *TWOT* #1708, #1709; *BDB* p. 94c. See also *Strong's* #905 (from #909).
11. George Ricker Berry, *The Interlinear Literal Translation of the Hebrew Old Testament* (Grand Rapids: Kregel Publications, 1975).
12. Katherine Bushnell says of this verse, "Had God simply meant by the words 'not good' that one person alone was not a desirable thing, the Hebrew expression for 'one alone' in Joshua 22:20; Isaiah 51:2, and others would seem more appropriate. This expression means, 'in-his-separation,' and from whom was Adam 'in separation' but from God?" *God's Word to Women*, was first published in 1911 under the title *Women's Correspondence Bible Class*; it first appeared under the present title in

1916. The last edition was printed in 1930. Recently it has been reprinted by God's Word to Women Publishers, P.O. Box 315, Mossville, IL 61552. See also Dana Hardwick, *O Thou Woman That Bringest Good Tidings—The Life and Work of Katherine C. Bushnell* (Saint Paul, Minn.: Christians for Biblical Equality, 1995) for an interesting biography.

Chapter 4

1. *TWOT* #1924a.
2. Neil Anderson and Charles Mylander, *The Christ-Centered Marriage* (Ventura, Calif.: Regal Books, 1996), p. 25.
3. *BDB* p. 179c.
4. Marvin R. Vincent, *Word Studies in the New Testament* (Peabody, Mass.: Hendrickson Publishers, nd.).
5. Let me qualify here that I am not saying there is only one woman for every man, and each must search until they find their "other half," or that perhaps one could marry the "wrong half," or some such thing. Nor am I saying that one must be married in order to be complete. I am saying that *the masculine in God's creation needs to be completed or helped by the feminine.* If married, completion is to begin in that relationship. Those who are not married get to skip this lesson and look directly to the corporate Church. All of us find our ultimate completion as we allow ourselves to be effectively knit together in the Body of Christ.
6. *TWOT* #1598a; *BDB* p. 740b. See also *Strong's* #5828.
7. *TWOT* #1598. Actually, "meet" translates two prepositions.
8. *TWOT* #1289; *BDB* p. 617. See also *Strong's* #5048, #5046.
9. *TWOT* #618; *BDB* p. 296a. See also *Strong's* #2332, #2331.
10. Donald Joy, *Relationships in the Image of God* (Nappanee, Ind.: Evangel Publishing House, 1996), p. 92.
11. Donald Joy, "Innate Differences Between Men and Women," "Focus on the Family Radio Program," 1993.
12. *TWOT* #1071a; *BDB* p. 523a,b. See also *Strong's* #3820 and #3824, "very widely used for feelings, the will and even the intellect; likewise the center of anything."
13. We want to emphasize here that marriage was not woman's only purpose, and her worth and design are not limited to that relationship. The Church itself needs the benefit of women's influence to fully express the image of God. Marriage was woman's initial purpose, however, and if married it is her primary calling.

Chapter 5

1. *Funk & Wagnalls Standard Reference Encyclopedia*, Vol. 25 (New York: Standard Reference Works Publishing Co., Inc.), p. 9265.

194   NOTES

2. Matthew Henry, *Commentary on the Whole Bible*, Vol. 6 (Grand Rapids: Fleming H. Revell Co., nd.), p. 562.

3. The *KJV, NKJV, NASB, RSV* and the *NRSV* essentially agree that Genesis 3:16 should read: "Your desire *shall be* for your husband, and he shall rule over you." However, the *NIV* and *CEV* read: "Your desire *will be* for your husband and he will rule over you." The different translations arise over a disagreement among scholars about whether to translate the controlling verb of the sentence *(mashal)* as a statement of fact, "he will rule"; or as a statement of wish or desired outcome, "he shall rule" or "let him rule." The *KJV, NKJV, NASB, RSV* and *NRSV* make a clear choice for a statement of wish or desired outcome. The *NIV* and *CEV* leave open the possibility of a dual interpretation. See *Gesenius' Hebrew Grammar, 2nd Edition,* edited by E. Kautzsch and A. E. Cowley (Oxford: Clarendon Press, 1910, [20th printing, 1990]), section 48b. See also *BDB* p. 605c.

The main contextual evidence in favor of "he shall rule" in Genesis 3:16 is just a few verses away in Genesis 4:7, where a parallel grammatical sequence and structure appear. God tells Cain, "(Sin's) *desire* is for you, but you *must master* ('rule') it." Genesis 4:7 would make no sense if God simply is telling Cain, "You will master/rule it," because the story makes it clear that Cain does not rule over sin, but sin rules over him, leading to the murder of his brother Abel. In the narrative, just as God had expressed a warning and a directive to Cain in Genesis 4:7, so in Genesis 3:16 God expresses a warning and a directive to Eve.

On the other hand, the parallelism in Genesis 3:16 and 4:7 is not perfectly exact. In Genesis 4:7 inanimate sin is likened to a person, while in 3:16 Eve is a living personality. In 4:7 sin is evil and absolutely opposed to God's rule, while in 3:16 Eve is fallen but redeemable. Further, from the context of 4:7 it is absolutely clear that God wants Cain to utterly master sin, to have no ongoing relationship with it. Obviously, this same instruction could not apply to Adam's relationship with his wife. God wants the husband and wife to be in intimate relationship with one another. In short, the context of 3:16 does not force the meaning "shall rule" found in 4:7.

4. See *Strong's* #8669. In the three places in the Old Testament where *teshuqah* occurs, it is clear from the context of these passages that in each case *teshuqah* indicates "desire to have hold of, desire to have complete possession of." Song of Solomon 7:10 (7:11 in Hebrew) bears this meaning with the connotation of the sexual desire appropriate within marriage; Genesis 4:7 bears this meaning with the connotation of sin's desire to entirely control Cain and cause him to do evil; and Genesis 3:16 bears this meaning in the woman's desire to "possess her husband." Both Genesis verses (Gen. 3:16; 4:7), closely related by grammar and context, indicate inappropriate desire. See also *BDB* p. 1003b,c and *TWOT* #2352a.

5. At issue is whether the root *shuq* means "stretching out after, longing,

desire" (*Strong's* #8669; "desire, longing"; *BDB* p. 1003c) or is homonymous with a *shuq* that has a different meaning, "to run after or over" (*Strong's* #7783); or "to overflow" (*BDB* p. 1003b, *shuq* 2nd meaning).

The question becomes further complicated by the fact that the earliest translations of the Hebrew Bible (see next endnote) possibly presuppose a textual variant, the Hebrew word, *teshubah*, and a different root, *shub*, which only differ from *teshuqah* and *shuq* by one letter. The root *shub* means "to return, turn back" or "to return again, turn back again" (*BDB* p. 996d, p. 1003c).

6. The Septuagint (the authorized Greek version of the Bible in Jesus' time), the Peshitta (5th century A.D. translation of the Bible into Syriac), the Samaritan Pentateuch, the Old Latin (4th century and before), the Sahidic Coptic (2nd century A.D.), the Bohairic Coptic (6th-7th centuries A.D.), the Armenian (5th century A.D.), and the Ethiopic (4th-5th centuries) all translate *teshuqah* (or *teshubah*, see previous note) in Genesis 3:16; 4:7 and Song of Solomon 7:10 as "turning" (*God's Word to Women* paragraphs 130-145).

7. *God's Word to Women* paragraph 130. Bushnell's argument is that because the Septuagint translates Genesis 3:16 and 4:7 as *apostrophe* (*apo*, "away from" + *strophe*, "turning, return" *BAGD* pp. 100, 86, 771) and Song of Solomon 7:10 as *epistrophe* (*epi*, "toward" + *strophe*, "turning, return" *BAGD* pp. 289b, 301), so should we.

8. "Harborview debates issue of circumcision of Muslim girls," Carol M. Ostrom, staff reporter, *Seattle Times* (September 13, 1996): 1.

Chapter 6

1. Dr. Reed Davis, Crista Counseling Radio Program, KCIS, Seattle, Wash., November 10, 1989.

2. Fromke, *Intention*, p. 11.

3. Larry Crabb, *The Marriage Builder* (Grand Rapids: Zondervan Publishing House, 1982), p. 48.

4. Fromke, *Intention*, p. 69.

Chapter 7

1. George Guilder, *Men and Marriage* (Gretna, La.: Pelican Publishing Co. Inc., 1986), p. 5.

2. *BAGD* p. 403-4; *TDNT* 3:605, 415. See also *Strong's* #2588.

3. *BAGD* p. 349c; see also *Strong's* #2272.

4. *BAGD* p. 727c; see also *Strong's* #4423 and #4072.

5. John and Paula Sandford, *The Transformation of the Inner Man* (South Plainfield, N.J.: Bridge Publishing, Inc., nd.), pp. 217-218.

6. John Powell, *Will the Real Me Please Stand Up* (Allen, Tex.: Tabor Publishing, 1985), p. 12.

7. John Powell, (printed source unknown).
8. Daphne Rose Kingma, *The Men We Never Knew* (Berkeley, Calif.: Conrai Press, 1993), p. 53.

Chapter 8

1. Hayford, *Spirit-Filled Life Bible*, p. 710.
2. *TDNT* 2:71, 150; *BAGD* p. 182, 181; see also *Strong's* #1225, #1228.
3. Marie Powers, *Shame, Thief of Intimacy* (Edmonds, Wash.: Aglow International, 1996), p. 26.
4. Terry Hershey, *Go Away, Come Closer* (Dallas, Tex.: Word Publishers, 1990), p. x.
5. Larry Crabb, *The Silence of Adam* (Grand Rapids: Zondervan Publishing, 1995), p. 184.
6. *The Interlinear Bible*, Jay P. Greene Sr., General Editor and Translator (Peabody, Mass.: Hendrickson Publishers, 1984).
7. Nancy Groom, *Married Without Masks* (Colorado Springs: NavPress, 1989), pp. 112-115.

Chapter 9

1. Herbert Lockyer, *All the Women of the Bible* (Grand Rapids,: Zondervan Publishing House, nd.), p. 270.
2. Ibid., p. 250.
3. *TWOT* #1407; *BDB* p. 665c; see also *Strong's* #5341.
4. *BAGD* p. 349; see also *Strong's* #2272.
5. *TWOT* #233; see also *Strong's* #982.
6. Fran Lance and Pat King, *Healing the Wounds of Women* (Seattle, Wash.: Free Lance Ministries, 1989), p. 88.
7. Hayford, *Spirit-Filled Life Bible*, p. 1160.
8. *TWOT* #1022.
9. *BDB* p. 738b; see also *Strong's* #5797, #5810.
10. *TWOT* #1496b
11. *TWOT* #1905c; *BDB* p. 965d; see also *Strong's* #7832.
12. *TWOT* #1673c; *BDB* p. 782d; see also *Strong's* #6106.
13. *TWOT* #1608a; *BDB* p. 742c; see also *Strong's* #5850, #5849.
14. *TWOT* #1071a; *BDB* p. 523a; see also *Strong's* #3820, #3824.
15. *TWOT* #2437.

Chapter 10

1. *The American Heritage Dictionary of the English Language*, Third Edition (Boston, Mass.: Houghton Mifflin Co., 1992), Electronic Version.
2. Dutch Sheets, *Intercessory Prayer* (Ventura, Calif.: Regal Books, 1996), p. 25.

3. Paul Billheimer, *Destined to Overcome* (Minneapolis: Bethany House, 1982), p. 24.

4. Although not a verbatim quote, the thought is contained in Paul Billheimer, *Destined for the Throne* (Fort Washington, Pa.: Christian Literature Crusade, 1975).

5. *TWOT* #624; *BDB* p. 298c; see also *Strong's* #2428.

6. *TWOT* #624; *BDB* p. 298c; see also *Strong's* #2342.

7. *TWOT* #255; *BDB* p. 124a; see also *Strong's* #1129.

8. *TWOT* #1022a.

9. *Strong's* #3027.

10. *BDB* p. 840c; see also *Strong's* #676.

11. Fromke, *The Ultimate Intention*, p. 10.

12. Exodus 28:1-6, Revelation 1:6. Purple robes refer to royalty or king's robes throughout Scripture. "'He has made us kings and priests' is clearly a present tense reference to the believer's function *now*, in witness and in worship." *Spirit-Filled Life Bible*, p. 1960.

Chapter 11

1. Bob Sorge, *The Fire of Delayed Answers* (Canandaigua, N.Y.: Oasis House, 1996), p. 41.

2. Lockyer, *Women*, Introduction.

3. Arthur Matthews, *Born for Battle* (Published jointly by Overseas Missionary Fellowship and Send the Light Trust; New York: Banta Co., 1978), p. 165.

4. Hayford, *Spirit-Filled Life Bible*, p. 431.

Chapter 12

1. Hayford, *Spirit-Filled Life Bible*, p. 1381.

2. James Dobson, *Straight Talk to Men and Their Wives* (Dallas, Tex.: Word Publishing, 1980), pp. 21, 22.

3. Harold Lindsell, Ph.D., DD., Editor, *Harper Study Bible* (Grand Rapids: Zondervan Bible Publishers, 1971), p. 1427.

4. David Blankenhorn, *Fatherless America* (New York: Basic Books, A division of HarperCollins, 1995), p. 1.

5. William Bennett, *Wall Street* Journal, date unknown.

6. Aleksandr Solzhenitsyn, printed source unknown.

7. Robert Bork, *Slouching Towards Gomorrah* (New York: Regan Books, A division of HarperCollins, 1996), p. 2.

8. Ibid., p. 193.

9. Blankenhorn, *Fatherless America*, p. 2.

10. Francis Frangipane, *The Days of His Presence* (Cedar Rapids, Ia.: Arrow Publications, 1995), p. 16.

11. Dobson, *Straight Talk*, p. 157.

12. John Powell, *Why Am I Afraid to Tell You Who I Am?* (Chicago: Argus Communications Co., 1969), p. 25, adapted.

13. Ibid., p. 5.

14. I must qualify here that none of what I have said is meant to imply that singles are excluded from functioning in the Church with equal power and developmental skill as marrieds. Certainly God has other methods of bringing us into spiritual and emotional maturity. However, the "norm" (as in "common method") for such development is within marriage. If one is married it is the height of deception to think that marriage and family can be ignored or skipped over and spiritual and emotional wholeness can be achieved on another level.

    We can be wonderfully eloquent, have great Bible knowledge, powerful personal charisma that can bring crowds to their feet or move them to tears and even appear to serve others with great self-sacrifice, yet all of it can be nothing more than polished, talented, self-serving "flesh."

    We can be emotionally vulnerable in men's or women's "accountability" groups, but if that intimacy and accountability does not carry over into the marriage in even greater measure, we are still fooling ourselves.

    Unless we are being real and vulnerable in our own homes, each serving and giving ourselves to our own spouse and family, we are yet playing the game of self-protectiveness. Our true spiritual development will remain stunted and we will continue to fall short of God's original design.

Chapter 13

1. N. Hillyer, Revision Editor, *New Bible Dictionary, Second Edition* (Leicester, England: InterVarsity Press, and Wheaton, Ill.: Tyndale House Publishers, 1962), p. 637.

2. *BDB* p. 184b; see also *Strong's* #1683, #1682.

3. *BDB* p. 180; see also *Strong's* #1696.

4. Samuel Prideaux Tregelles, Translator, *Gesenius Hebrew and Chaldee Lexicon* (Grand Rapids: Baker Book House, nd.), #1696 (5).

5. Although verse 9 says that Barak will get "no glory," 1 Samuel 12:9-11 credits him with delivering Israel out of the hand of Sisera and the armies of Hazor. He did not get the glory of delivering the death blow to Sisera, but the honor for the victory of the battle was obviously a shared one. ("Bedan" in 1 Samuel 12:11 is Barak. See *RSV, NEB* and margins of other translations.)

6. *The Bethany Parallel Commentary* (Minneapolis, Minn.: Bethany House, 1985), quote by Matthew Henry, p. 449.

7. *BAGD* p. 115; see also *Strong's* #769.

8. *The Bethany Parallel Commentary*, quote by G. Campbell Morgan, p. 428.
9. *The Bethany Parallel Commentary*, N.T., quote by Matthew Henry, p. 249.
10. Junia, so rendered in the *KJV, NKJV, NRSV* and margins of other translations, is a feminine name. Various other translations render it "Junias," which is masculine. "Although the gender of Junia(s) is questioned, early commentators took the name to be feminine, which is consistent with Greek and Latin literature of the first century. The name (Junia) was a very common one in Rome, though the masculine form 'Junias' was not attested." St. John Chrysostom, in the fourth century, obviously recognized Junia as feminine when he declared, "O how great is the devotion of this woman." Catherine Clark Kroeger, Mary Evans, Elaine Storkey, Editors, *Study Bible for Women, the New Testament* (Grand Rapids: Baker Books, 1995).
11. Phoebe was called a "servant" in the church in Cenchrea (see Rom. 16:1,2), but the word in Greek is *diakonos*—deacon. Scholars generally agree that Phoebe held an official position as deacon of the church at Cenchrea. She is also called a "helper" in verse 2. The word in Greek is *prostatis*. The verbal equivalent of *prostatis* is *proistemi*, which describes the governing action of "overseers," etc., in Romans 12:8; 1 Thessalonians 5:12; 1 Timothy 3:4,5,12; 5:17; Titus 3:8,14. Paul instructed the whole church at Rome (men and women) to "receive her in the Lord in a manner worthy of the saints, and assist her in whatever business she has need of."
12. *The Bethany Parallel Commentary*, O.T., quote from Matthew Henry, p. 1542.
13. Randy Phillips, "The Power of a Promise Kept," KIRO TV, April 4, 1997.
14. Ken R. Canfield, "Lutheran Brotherhood," *Bond Publication* (Fall 1992).
15. Josh McDowell, weekly radio program, quote by Dave McCoombs, May 1994.

What Is Aglow International?

—⁓—

From one nation to 135 worldwide...
From one fellowship to over 3,300...
From 100 women to more than 2 million...

Aglow International has experienced phenomenal growth since
its inception 30 years ago. In 1967, four women from the state
of Washington prayed for a way to reach out to other Christian
women in simple fellowship, free from denominational boundaries.

—⁓—

The first meeting held in Seattle, Washington, USA, drew more
than 100 women to a local hotel. From that modest beginning,
Aglow International has become one of the largest intercultural,
interdenominational women's organizations in the world.

—⁓—

Each month, Aglow touches the lives of an estimated two million women on six continents through local fellowship meet-
ings, Bible studies, support groups, retreats, conferences and various outreaches. From the inner city to the upper echelons, from
the woman next door to the corporate executive, Aglow seeks to
minister to the felt needs of women around the world.

—⁓—

Christian women find Aglow a "safe place" to grow spiritually
and begin to discover and use the gifts, talents and abilities God
has given them. Aglow offers excellent leadership training and
varied opportunities to develop those leadership skills.

—⁓—

Undergirding the evangelistic thrust of the ministry is an emphasis on prayer, which has led to an active prayer network linking
six continents. The vast prayer power available through Aglow
women around the world is being used by God to influence
countless lives in families, communities, cities and nations.

Aglow's Mission Statement

Our mission is to lead women to Jesus Christ and provide opportunity for Christian women to grow in their faith and minister to others.

—⚉—

Aglow's Continuing Focus...

- To reconcile woman to her womanhood as God designed. To strengthen and empower her to fulfill the unfolding plan of God as He brings restoration to the male/female relationship, which is the foundation of the home, the church and the community.
- To love women of all cultures with a special focus on Muslim women.
- To reach out to every strata of society, from inner cities to isolated outposts to our own neighborhoods, with very practical and tangible expressions of the love of Jesus.

—⚉—

Gospel Light and Aglow International present an important new series of Bible studies for use in small groups. The first two studies in the Aglow Bible Study Series, **Shame: Thief of Intimacy** *and* **Keys to Contentment**, *will be available through Gospel Light in the spring of 1998. For information about these and other outstanding Bible study resources from Aglow, call Gospel Light at 1-800-4-GOSPEL.*

Aglow Ministers In...

Albania, Angola, Anguilla, Antigua, Argentina, Aruba, Australia, Austria, Bahamas, Barbados, Belgium, Belize, Benin, Bermuda, Bolivia, Botswana, Brazil, British Virgin Islands, Bulgaria, Burkina Faso, Cameroon, Canada, Cayman Islands, Chile, China, Colombia, Congo (Rep. of), Congo (Dem. Rep. of), Costa Rica, Côte d'Ivoire, Cuba, Curaçao, Czech Republic, Denmark, Djibouti, Dominica, Dominican Republic, Ecuador, Egypt, El Salvador, England, Equatorial Guinea, Estonia, Ethiopia, Faroe Islands, Fiji, Finland, France, Gabon, the Gambia, Germany, Ghana, Greece, Grenada, Guam, Guatemala, Guinea, Guyana, Haiti, Honduras, Hungary, Iceland, India, Indonesia, Ireland, Israel, Jamaica, Japan, Kazakstan, Kenya, Korea, Kyrgyzstan, Latvia, Malawi, Malaysia, Mali, Mauritius, Mexico, Fed. States of Micronesia, Mongolia, Montserrat, Mozambique, Myanmar, Nepal, Netherlands, Papua New Guinea, New Zealand, Nicaragua, Niger, Nigeria, Norway, Oman, Pakistan, Panama, Peru, Philippines, Portugal, Puerto Rico, Romania, Russia, Rwanda, Samoa (American), Samoa (Western), Scotland, Senegal, Sierra Leone, Singapore, South Africa, Spain, Sri Lanka, St. Kitts, St. Lucia, St. Maartan, St. Vincent, Sweden, Switzerland, Tajikistan, Tanzania, Thailand, Togo, Tonga, Trinidad/ Tobago, Turks & Caicos Islands, Uganda, Ukraine, United States, U.S. Virgin Islands, Uruguay, Uzbekistan, Venezuela, Vietnam, Wales, Yugoslavia, Zambia, Zimbabwe.
*One extremely restricted 10/40 Window nation.

How do I find my nearest Aglow Fellowship? Call or write us at:

AGLOW.
INTERNATIONAL

P.O. Box 1749, Edmonds, WA 98020-1749
Phone: (425) 775-7282 or 1-800-755-2456
Fax: (425) 778-9615   E-mail: aglow@aglow.org
Web site: http://www.aglow.org/